SEX SATISFACTION AND HAPPY MARRIAGE

A Note On the Author and His Work

The Author of the present volume, an Englishman residing in Canada these past fifty years, is best known as a writer and worker in the field of social service. He is a clergyman of the Protestant Episcopal (Anglican) Church. Most of his life has been spent in the mission-field where he encountered first-hand the personal problems of men and women in many varied phases of life.

In the course of his work he could not help but be tremendously impressed, again and again, with the vast number of ruined lives and homes that could be traced to some form of marital maladjustment, due either to ignorance or to a faulty concept of the sexual relationship. He became convinced that many of the tragedies he came to know about could have been avoided if the persons involved could have had the sex education necessary to enable them to achieve happy marriage.

The present manual is an attempt to supply the sexual knowledge that is essential for normal happy marriage. Since first issued in 1936 the book has made history as regards the nature of its acceptance. It is today recognized by authorities everywhere (see Critical Comments elsewhere herein) as one of the most valuable contributions ever made to the layman's literature dealing with the importance of the sexual element in achieving successful marriage. Not only the Press, but individuals, including physicians, clergymen, and the laity, have come forward to express approval. Voluntary letters from readers of the book eloquently attest its value in getting marriages off to a good start, as well as in salvaging marriages that have veered from the path of felicity.

It is to be hoped that with the current edition—completely revised under the close supervision of specializing physicians, eminent attorneys, a psychologist, an endocrinologist, a chemist, a literary adviser, and others—the usefulness of the work will be greater than ever.

SEX SATISFACTION
AND
HAPPY MARRIAGE

A practical handbook of sexual information to enable couples to achieve normal, happy marriage; intended for those married or about to be; also for use in their work by doctors, the clergy, social workers, lawyers, and others in the advisory professions, who may find recommendation of this book a convenient and time-saving method of imparting advice.

By the Reverend

ALFRED HENRY TYRER

Clergyman of the Protestant Episcopal (Anglican) Church

Foreword by

ROBERT L. DICKINSON, M.D.

EMERSON BOOKS, INCORPORATED
NEW YORK
1970

Legal Sanction for Sex Education

The courts of our country have wisely and generously gone on record as favoring rational sex education. They did this in the Stopes case (United States District Court), Federal Judge John M. Woolsey stating:

". . . as Professor William G. Sumner aptly used to say in his lectures on the Science of Society, at Yale, marriage, in its essence, is a status of antagonistic cooperation.

"In such a status, necessarily, centripetal and centrifugal forces are continuously at work, and the measure of its success obviously depends on the extent to which the centripetal forces are predominant.

"The book before me here has as its whole thesis the strengthening of the centripetal forces in marriage, and instead of being inhospitably received, it should, I think, be welcomed within our borders."

In the Dennett case (United States Circuit Court of Appeals) Federal Judge Augustus N. Hand found occasion to declare:

". . . The old theory that information about sex matters should be left to chance has greatly changed. . . . It may reasonably be thought that accurate information, rather than mystery and curiosity, is better in the long run."

Acknowledgments

I most gratefully acknowledge my deep indebtedness to Dr. Robert L. Dickinson, of New York, to Dr. Margaret Batt, of Toronto, and to Dr. F. N. Walker, of Toronto, for valuable criticisms and scientific data; also to Mrs. Francis Johnson and Professor J. F. Macdonald, of the University of Toronto, for valuable literary and other suggestions.

THE AUTHOR

Note to the Reader

It is the author's sincere request that no one glance here and there through this book and so attempt to appraise it. A wrong impression might possibly be so derived.

This book deals with the most intimate, and at the same time, the most sacred relationship between husband and wife, and in so doing speaks frankly and openly, as is necessary, for all who feel the need of help and instruction. The many lessons it teaches can be understood and appreciated only if every word be read thoughtfully and without skipping a single line.

CONTENTS

CONTENTS

Foreword

One who has watched and sincerely appreciated the many years of self-sacrificing endeavor on the part of this pioneer in marriage counseling welcomes the appearance of his teaching in the form of a book. It meets the particular need of people reared in that atmosphere of church homes that looks askance at almost all sex impulse or manifestation. The wording of it is such that, in the realm of sex education and medical information, it belongs in the new category—common in other fields of physical and mental hygiene—namely, the standard medical work adapted to the use of the laity.

Familiarity with the literature of this field, often called marriage hygiene, leads one to make comparisons and to offer the opinion that the Tyrer book is restrained and moderate, while embodying the gist of information in one aspect of life and behavior and attitude essential to happiness in marriage in any degree of completeness and harmony.

ROBERT L. DICKINSON, M.D.

New York

Preface

THIS book has its source in the fountain of bitter sorrow and the remembrance of scalding tears. Looking backward down the long corridors of silence and loneliness at the years that are gone, I realize how very different life might have been had the information contained in this book been given to me and my wife when we set out upon the great adventure of married life over forty years ago. But among our many friends there was none to come forward with wise counsel in the hour of our need. It is indeed one of the saddest tragedies in life that so few young people realize their need when they first set out. *By the time the need has manifested itself it may be too late.* The mariner seeks no assistance until his ship strikes the hidden rock; but the damage is done then and it *may* be irreparable.

My knowledge of this sad side of life, however, is derived from much more than any personal experience. A ministry in the Church of over forty years gave me, on many an occasion, a close-up view into homes where disaster had already occurred, or was on the verge of occurring. During the past eight years I have been engaged in marriage counseling and sex education, and this book is the immediate outcome of numerous letters of enquiry, and confidences that have come to me from married and unmarried men and women who have been facing problems that threaten their lives and homes with disaster. My answers to such letters have elicited such grateful thanks that I have felt compelled to put into book form what I consider to be the main facts that every married, and every engaged, couple ought to know.

It is, however, with a very deep sense of responsibility that I have undertaken this task. It is not an easy one. We of this generation are living in an hour of transition from the day when sex was considered as something to be hidden, something that had undefined relation to impurity, something the mention of which was absolutely "off color," to the cleaner, sweeter day that is dawning, when, next to life itself, it will be acknowledged openly, and exalted, as the most important thing in the world—that upon which the fulness and happiness of life depend, a thing God-given, sacred and legitimate in all its normal manifestations. But inasmuch as today is a period of transition, we must expect to find some people, mostly well-meaning and conscientious parents, still affected by the views of the day that is swiftly passing. To them, to the end of their lives probably, the very mention of sex will be taboo. Mistakenly imagining that they are guarding the virtue of their children by keeping them in ignorance, these parents resent any attempt to educate their offspring. To such parents arguments will in all probability be useless. All I can do is inform them kindly, and with sympathy, on the authority of the world's greatest teachers, from the Bible down to Havelock Ellis, Lord Dawson of Penn, Marie Stopes, Margaret Sanger, and a hundred other writers whose influence is making the world better and more beautiful, that the sexual life is essentially pure, and a thing to be gloried in; and that in millions of cases the attitude of taboo and reticence in regard to it has been a source of infinite sorrow and suffering. If parents would save their children from the likelihood of such experiences they must see to it that correct information concerning married life is made available. Otherwise if disaster should ever come, those parents may find themselves shedding tears of bitterness in the realization that the responsibility had been theirs, but they had failed to live up to it. God is reported in the Bible as saying "My people perish for lack of knowledge." Young people about to be married need knowledge. If it be denied them there is danger that they too may perish.

Happy sexual relationship between husbands and wives constitutes the chief cornerstone of the happy home. The sexual relationship however is too often anything but satisfactory, owing in many cases to mutual ignorance that might have been corrected very easily in the beginning. This fact is being realized more and more widely by intelligent people who keep an open mind. If parents do not feel able to give the education necessary, sound books, reverently written, are available.

Many such books on sex and marriage have been produced, but all that I have seen may be divided into two classes. The one is apt to be too extended, and consequently has to be published at a price that for many is prohibitive. The other, often in pamphlet form, is too brief, and only hints at matters that the authors seem to have been inhibited from discussing freely; thus leaving the reader too frequently just on the border of information that is most needed. The present volume will be found free from both these defects. Furthermore, while dealing primarily with sex, the book contains a long chapter—"Concerning Many Things" —in which advice is proffered along lines other than sexual, but having a direct bearing on the happiness and success of the married life.

Primarily this book is for the edification of young engaged couples. It is easier to avoid mistakes than to correct them, and many a marriage is ruined the first night, or during the honeymoon. It should be read very carefully by both—first separately, then together—and then discussed. The information it contains is sometimes more specifically for the benefit of the man, sometimes of the woman. This has induced me to address myself directly to the one or the other as occasion required. Being essentially a guide-book, in which after the first reading particular chapters will be re-read for particular information, reiteration has been necessary.

A realization of the true place and meaning and beauty of the wholesome and normal sex life will never be reached by anyone so long as its physical manifestations (whatever technique be adopted) are considered to belong to a supposedly low and animal side of our nature, as opposed to a high spiritual side. The joys of married life, springing from mutual love and desire, should not be subjected to scurrilous suggestion of materialism or animality. It is not true that some of the natural expressions and manifestations of life are sacred and spiritual, and some material and earthly. They all originate from the same source, which is "God," or "Nature," or whatever term one's philosophy leads one to adopt. Nourishing the body by taking physical food, for instance, is just as sacred a process (no more, no less) as nourishing the mind by following intellectual pursuits, or nourishing the emotional nature through religious concepts and practices, or revelling in things beautiful to eye and ear. There is nothing about the sexual organs, or their functions, to be ashamed of, or bashful about; nothing that places them in a different category from the digestive organs or any other part of our anatomy. Prudery has reaped a sufficiently disastrous harvest in the past and it needs to be rebuked.

With some of the ancients it was the custom, we are told, for the newly married couple to spend the first night, and pass through their first marital experience, within the sacred walls of their temples, and in the presence of their gods. Perhaps they had a deeper and clearer vision of truth than we moderns. So the following pages will not be cluttered up with repeated attempts to impress on the reader that there is a spiritual side to true marriage. That is assumed throughout. Every ardent sexual impulse, in its legitimate and natural manifestation springing out of love, is as sacred as any other human activity, and this book is an attempt so to present it.

St. Paul tells us (if any need to be told) that "marriage is honorable in all": and then he adds "and the bed undefiled." He is right about marriage, but mistaken in suggesting that the marriage bed is always undefiled. It is defiled too often because of deplorable ignorance of sexual matters, and of the requirements of a natural and satisfactory sex life. If this book succeeds in starting aright one young couple who would otherwise miss the way, or if it succeeds in correcting some unsatisfactory condition that has already arisen, and, in so doing, re-establishes happiness in even a single home, it will not have been written in vain.

A.H.T.

Toronto

Introduction

SUPPOSE some possible inhabitant of the planet Mars, without the slightest resemblance to a human being, and perhaps sexless, succeeded in making a journey to the earth, and wished to take back for the edification of Martian physiologists and psychologists a specimen of us earth-dwellers. Suppose further that the available means of transportation would admit of only one passenger. Would a man or a woman be chosen to represent humanity? With the keen intelligence and powers of observation that must be conceded any being capable of making such an interplanetary trip, our visitor would recognize very clearly that neither a man nor a woman could be considered as an adequate specimen on which to form generalizations regarding the whole race. The male possesses characteristics not found in the female, and the female possesses characteristics not found in the male, and the special characteristics of one could not be inferred by any psychologist from an observation of the other. The differences are not only physical, but mental and emotional and (for lack of a more definite and generally intelligible word) spiritual. No one man and no one woman could be found who, in his or her own person, would possess all the qualities to be found in both. A thorough and complete understanding and generalization regarding humanity, with all its potentialities, could be obtained only by a blending or synthesis of both sexes. Whatever completeness is possible in humanity—whatever the sum total of its predictable potentialities—the elements of such a calculation can be found in neither man nor woman, but only in a unification of both.

The nearest approach to a complete blending of two personalities into one perfect entity, which must embody both male and female elements, is the ideal marriage, in which a man and a woman come together under the influence of mutual love, and undertake by solemn vows to forsake all others, and to cherish, comfort and honor each the other, for better, for worse, in sickness and in health, until death shall end the partnership. This is ideal marriage. It involves mutual love, respect and admiration, lifelong companionship, mutual sympathy and mutual strengthening in all the trials of life, mutual consideration always of each other's every need—physical, mental and emotional. "And they two shall become one flesh" facing life and its problems boldly, fighting its battles, enjoying its pleasures, cherishing the same aspirations and hopes, with a mutual sense of duty to the society of which they form an integral part. Such a life, and such a life only, with, of course, its foundation of a perfectly satisfactory sex life, constitutes true marriage—a unifying of two bodies and minds and souls, from which unification there shall spring a progeny to carry on and on towards the better and happier world of a day still to come.

I do not think this is too idealistic a concept of marriage. I believe that monogamous marriage, to which both parties are faithful through life, is the only possible basis of a permanently stable and happy home, and that such a home is the only foundation of any sound human society. And I believe that "Nature," or "God," (again according to philosophical concept) supports this view. Nature lures the feet of the young into the pathway that leads to monogamous marriage. It is the pathway of romantic love, and she does not delay long in inviting her children to tread the way. Young people passing out of childhood into maturity realize, sooner or later, that life is being lit up by feelings and emotions never experienced before. They have observed their bodies undergoing noticeable changes that have been more or less intriguing, and with the maturing of their sex organs a new and vital interest develops that adds to the zest of life. Companions of the opposite sex become more and more interesting, and, if nature is allowed to run a true course, sooner or later some romantic love will come into life—love, in comparison with which all other interests, for the time being, take second place. Nature's call for a mate is dominant: "It is not good for man that he should be alone." So, lest the race should perish, she has given her creatures the impelling force of ardent sexual desire that leads lovers to assume the responsibilities of married life.

In the life of love that marriage implies, satisfactory sexual intercourse is the prime factor. If it be unsatisfactory, then in that very fact the marriage is a failure. There are, of course, many other factors besides sex that are necessary for a successful marriage, but they are all secondary. They may all be present in the fullest degree, but if the accompanying sex life is definitely unsatisfactory, they will be powerless to create the happiness that must underlie all home life if it is to be successful.

Unfortunately few marriages are ideal—some being destitute of one essential element and some of another. It is however on the sexual side of the union that most disasters occur. Where there is mutual love, and sympathy, and a reasonable power of mutual adaptation, together with industry that provides a proper setting, then with an adequate knowledge of sex anatomy and sex technique, together with a right mental attitude, marriage may be ideal from the first night of the honeymoon for as long as life may last.

It is however a sad fact that many young couples meet with disaster after marriage, although they may have entered into the companionship with the highest ideals and hopes, and with everything promising for success and happiness. The wedding ceremony over, they set sail joyously on the intriguing sea of matrimony believing there is some wonderful port of happiness ahead—as indeed there may be if they will but guide their bark aright. Relatives and friends see them off after flooding them with presents and good wishes; but, strangely, in ninety-nine cases out of a hundred it never seems to occur to those interested in the newly-weds to provide them with the one thing in all the world they need most as they set out on their voyage—*a chart to show them the way.* For there are hidden rocks and treacherous shoals in the sea of matrimony, and its shores are strewn with the wreckage of abandoned hopes and ruined homes and lives. But do not fear. Those rocks and shoals need cause no anxiety in the minds of intelligent lovers who are willing to learn. Through the long ages of human experience the main points of danger have all been discovered and charted, and simple wisdom, and thoughtful care, and the exercise of some degree of common sense will make the voyage safe and sure.

It seems to be an almost universal supposition that instinct is a sufficient guidance for young couples on their entry into married life. It is not. Instinct is quite sufficient in the lower animal world where sympathy and understanding as known to us, do not exist; where there is no esthetic sense; where love in its highest and deepest sacramental meaning is unknown; and where there has been no false education to produce unnatural inhibitions and repressions. But men and women in their sexual relationship, as in their mental and emotional reactions, are in a totally different category from the lower animals. Human love, when it expresses itself in mutual sexual ministrations, may open up a world not only of higher physical gratification, but also of emotional and psychical joy, of which the animals apparently know nothing. Love in its physical manifestations and technique is an art. Those who refuse to recognize it as such and who scorn the idea of any instruction in its intimate details are probably headed for disaster.

There were more than a million divorces on this continent within the past five years. This fact, however, does not begin to tell the whole story of marital failure. In addition to the divorces obtained, there are the hundreds of thousands of couples who would be divorced if finances or other circumstances permitted; there are the innumerable couples who have found relief from an impossible married life in legal separations, or by simply living apart without bothering to go through any legal formality; and finally there is the vast number of marriages where the breaking point has not been quite reached but where discord and dissension poison the daily atmosphere and make the home anything but the haven of rest and love it ought to be.

What is the cause of all this trouble, and what the cure? This is certainly one of the most important questions facing the world today. We are told, often enough, that the home is the foundation of our whole social structure. It is. But the home itself, to be secure, must be built on a foundation of loving and happy companionship. If that foundation disintegrates, the home itself topples, and with the destruction of the home the whole social fabric is shaken. Anyone who does anything towards lessening domestic unhappiness, and towards strengthening the bonds that bind homes together, is doing the world a very real service.

The object of this book is to furnish a chart for those who are about to start out in married life. If they will study it seriously and take its admonitions to heart they may find married life as wonderful and beautiful as they ever imagined it. If the book falls into the hands of some couple who have already lost their way, it may help them re-establish their course, encourage them to set their sails afresh and, with renewed hope, search on for the promised land of which they used to dream in their courtship days. If, with a new vision and understanding, they are wise and careful, they may yet come safely to port—and find life still worth living.

Chapter I

THE PHYSICAL SIDE OF MARRIAGE

THERE is no institution in human society of greater importance than the institution of marriage. Whether or not the Biblical account in Genesis be considered as having any historical significance, it very certainly sets forth an intelligent and sublime appreciation of the primal importance and the sacredness of the sexual relationship, and it is a sufficient rebuke to the prudery that looks askance at any mention or manifestation of sex and its impulses. In the Paradise of God there presented, the Lord God Himself brings the woman to the arms of the man, recognizing his need of a sexual companion, and we are told:

> *"Therefore shall a man leave his father and his mother and shall cleave unto his wife, and they shall be one flesh. And they were both naked, the man and his wife, and were not ashamed."*
>
> (GENESIS, Chap. ii, 24, 25)

The thoughtful consideration of that inspired concept of the sexual relationship should banish from our minds forever all trace of prudery and shame in connection with it.

Without wholesome and happy marriage there cannot be a wholesome and happy state. Without a satisfactory sex life there cannot be a happy and successful marriage. The sex life of the human race thus takes on an importance than which there would seem to be nothing much greater. The life of the world depends on it. In order that her creatures shall not be indifferent to its demands, Nature has made the act of sexual intercourse the supreme physical pleasure of life—a pleasure which at its climax may, at times, almost reach a point of ecstasy. To attain this climax, which is the rightful heritage of every married couple, at least three things are necessary: (1) There must be an adequate understanding of the sex organs and of their proper functioning; (2) There must be a correct mental attitude (most important for the wife)—an attitude that harbors no inhibitions, no repressions, no fears and which thus admits of a complete abandonment to the joys of the sexual embrace; (3) There must be a sympathetic appreciation of the needs of each other.

These necessary conditions are not always present, and when they are absent it is more often the wife who is disappointed than the husband. He invariably reaches his climax, or orgasm, while she may never do so. Some couples go through life without ever knowing that the wife is even capable of an orgasm. And the sexual embrace in which the wife fails to experience an orgasm can never be as satisfactory as it should be to the husband, for the true lover always finds his own joy increased by the realization that he is producing an ecstatic experience for his mate.

Inhibitions, which have been mentioned above and which affect the attitude of the mind towards sexual enjoyment, are more common with wives than husbands. They are very largely the result of early training. A strong and quite natural and desirable sexual impulse in either husband or wife, which might lead to a joyous experience and mutual satisfaction, and to an intensification of love, may be completely inhibited and repressed, by, for instance, a vague belief and fear that it is just some part of a lower animal nature, and that it is really a sin to give way to it. Such fears have been grafted into the minds of tens of thousands of people by a false religious idealism. As a matter of fact the *real sin lies in the repression*. Sex desire is as natural as the desire for food when one is hungry, and its satisfaction is just as pure and quite as sacred as any of the other phenomena of life. Whoever deprecates it as something to be renounced, repressed or resisted, is flinging back in Nature's face her most delightful gift.

The false religious idealism that has presumed to exalt celibacy as a higher and more holy state than matrimony has been responsible for millions of wrecked homes and blasted lives. For centuries upon centuries that idealism has suggested to the minds of ignorant

27

and susceptible people that there is something inherently low and degrading in sex and its manifestations —something to be more or less ashamed of, something impure. A saner view, however, is growing in the minds of intelligent people, and the saner view is not irreligious. True practical religion, dissociated from man-made theology and man-made creeds, may be a very real and beautiful thing, necessary to the world's well-being and happiness. It surely is. But repudiation of sex is certainly no part of it. Whatever a person's idea of "God" may be, it is certain that sex is the plan and purpose of that God, and religion will never come into its own until it has vision to see that *there is absolutely no virtue in virginity that may not be present in the most ecstatic moment of the sexual embrace in marriage*. To deny this would be to deny the sacredness of the desire for parenthood.

The cumulative effect of the false religious teachings in regard to sex in the past has resulted in what may be called the tradition of reticence. In the average home today, any slightest allusion to sex is taboo. When the natural curiosity of children prompts them to ask questions, silly lies are told them. And they soon begin to suspect it. They observe that those about them never allow themselves to be seen naked. They are cautioned against letting themselves be seen naked, and it is suggested that there is something improper about it. If they are seen touching their sexual organs they are rebuked, perhaps punished, but they are told nothing

28

except that it is "very naughty," which doesn't prevent them from continuing the examination when there is no one around. Any information (or misinformation) they accumulate is usually imparted to them in guilty whispers by some slightly more sophisticated companion. In their homes they observe that any of the bodily organs other than the sex organs are discussed at any time, and they grow up with an ingrained idea that sex is something to be hidden—that no question about it is permissible. The ultimate result of all this is that, in millions of cases the world over, young couples come face to face with the mysteries and problems of sex for the first time on their marriage night; and as might be expected, tens of thousands of them make an utter failure of what ought to be an exquisite experience and as a result, suffer, perhaps for the rest of their lives. There is only one remedy for all this, and that is *knowledge*.

Chapter II

THE FEMALE SEX ORGANS

THE general facts about one's sex organs ought to be known to everyone. There is no more practical way of obtaining this knowledge than by a careful examination of one's own body. By the use of a hand mirror a girl can see the relative position of the different parts. There is nothing wrong about making such an examination; indeed it is a very wise thing for every girl to do intelligently and thoroughly before she gets married, or when she gets curious about her body, whatever her age. Ignorance never gets anyone anywhere—except into trouble. The illustration on page 31 will help in this examination.

First of all, there are the large outer lips, or labia (as the medical books call them) which are covered with hair. The main function of these lips is to be a protection to the more delicate parts within. These inner parts are, first, the two smaller lips covered with a dull pinkish and very delicate skin. At the upper extremity of these inner lips there will be found a little fold of membrane and a slight prominence that is known as the clitoris. Though it is small it is a very important part of the sex organism of a woman, and corresponds to the penis in the man. It is endowed with very delicate and

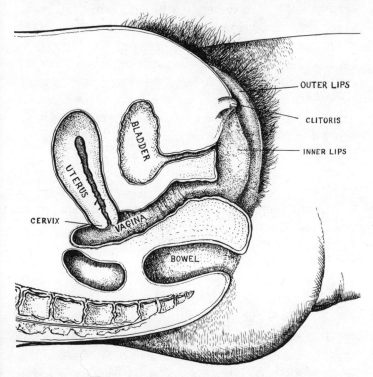

sensitive nerve tissue and responds to the caresses of her lover, swelling up and becoming hard, as does his penis; and just as the head of the penis is the center of pleasure for a man, so the clitoris in a woman is the focal point of her greatest external enjoyment. The independent stimulation and caressing of the clitoris is necessary in many women before they can arrive at their climax, or orgasm. All this, however, will be dealt with further on.

An inch or so below the clitoris is the entrance to the bladder, but it is a very small opening and will not be easily detected. It is of no importance, however, as far as the sex life is concerned and therefore needs no more consideration here. Just below this is the entrance to the vagina—the passage where intercourse between husband and wife takes place. Before the consummation of marriage (the first act of intercourse) this passage is partly closed by what is called the hymen, which will be dealt with in another paragraph. The vagina is from three to five inches deep and is completely closed at the upper end. Towards the further end of the passage and on the upper side of it there will be found the cervix, or neck of the uterus, or womb, which projects into the vagina. Its correct position ought to be known to every woman and it can be determined by feeling for it with her finger. Perhaps the best position for her to take in making this exploration is to squat down till the body is resting on the calves of the legs which, of course, must be separated. An easier position perhaps is to stand with one foot on the floor and the other resting on a chair, separating the thighs as widely as possible. The cervix will be noticed as a domelike projection about the size of a small walnut, smooth and firm, with a very slight depression in the center. This depression is the mouth of the womb, or uterus, and it is through this small opening that sperms from the male have to pass before pregnancy can take place. At the time of child-birth this opening stretches sufficiently for the child to be born. In a woman who has never had a baby the mouth of the uterus is very small. After the stretching at childbirth it soon returns to something like its previous state, though not quite, and successive births

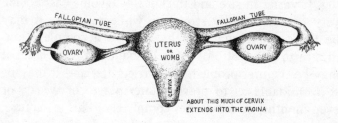

tend to enlarge it still more. For this reason a woman generally becomes pregnant more easily after she has had her first baby. The distance up the vagina to the cervix varies in different women, of course, but it is usually about three and a half to four inches.

The uterus, or womb, as is shown in the illustration above is a pear-shaped organ. It is, of course, only the extreme lower portion of it, which projects into the vagina, that can be felt. Into the large upper end, two tubes enter, one from each side. They are called the Fallopian tubes and they connect the uterus with the ovaries in which the eggs are developed. In the chapter

"Where Babies Come From" there will be found a fuller description of these organs and their functions.

The hymen, or "maidenhead" as it is sometimes called, and which has already been referred to, is a structure covered with mucous membrane; and, until it has been either stretched or nicked, it partly closes the entrance to the vagina in virgin girls—as a rule. *I say as a rule.* It must be distinctly understood that it is not invariably present in virgins. Its absence signifies nothing. It varies in size and thickness—in some cases being very thin and easily stretched, while in others it may be thick and tough enough to prove a complete hindrance to penetration by the husband. In such cases it may be the first problem of married life, and it may be so formidable as to prevent intercourse for weeks, or even months, or sometimes completely. This, of course, would be very unusual and medical advice should be sought. Accordingly it is my strong advice to every girl to see to it that her hymen is sufficiently stretched before her marriage. She can do this by gently introducing two fingers over a period of a couple of weeks and then begin to use three fingers. There is absolutely nothing wrong, indelicate or in the least degree objectionable in doing this, and it may save a great deal of trouble. A physician's advice might be helpful in this matter.

Chapter III

THE MALE SEX ORGANS

THE male sex organs consist of the penis and the testicles on the outside, together with several important glands inside the body. The penis overhangs the testicles at the lower part of the trunk, which in this region, like the female body, is covered with the short hair that makes its first appearance at the time of puberty, or maturity. The penis is a cylindrical body which, when no sexual stimulation is present, is three or four inches in length and an inch or so in thickness. Beneath the outer skin it is composed of a soft, fleshy, spongy tissue that is capable of considerable expansion. A flow of blood to the parts, which occurs when there is any sexual stimulation, makes the organ enlarge and become hard and stiff; and, instead of hanging limp, it becomes erect, standing out at an acute angle to the body. This condition, in which it becomes about six inches in length, and one and a quarter to one and a half inches thick, is called erection, and it is, of course, a necessary condition before intercourse with a female can take place. When the organ does not respond to stimulation, but remains limp under conditions that ought to affect it, the condition is called impotence, which will be dealt with in a later chapter. The head of the penis, which is called the *glans,* is a little larger than the body of the organ. The head, or glans, is normally covered up by a continuation of the outer skin of the penis. This continuation is called the foreskin, or prepuce, and it serves as a protection to the more delicate surface of the glans. This foreskin can be drawn back (and under normal conditions it will be drawn, or pushed, back during intercourse) thus leaving the head bare, the outer surface of which is a soft, delicate, pink membrane that is supplied with an abundance of extremely sensitive nerves which make it the center point of sensitivity during intercourse. This head, like the rest of the penis, enlarges and hardens under the increased blood supply that rushes automatically to the whole sex-region when adequate stimulation is present. In some men this foreskin that covers the head of the penis is excessively long, and sometimes it cannot be retracted; or, if retracted, it may be with the accompaniment of pain. When any of these abnormal conditions are present, a very simple operation called circumcision, in which the superfluous skin is removed, may be necessary.

The testicles are two firm, oblong, glandular bodies lying close to the inner parts of the thighs just below the penis, and they are enclosed in a sac of soft skin called the scrotum. It is in the testicles that the *spermatozoa* are produced. These spermatozoa are very active

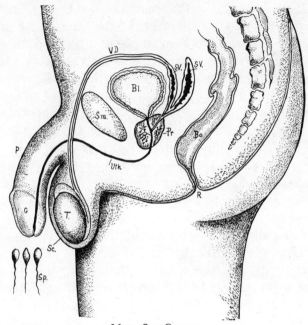

MALE SEX ORGANS

P.—Penis.
G.—Glans: Head of penis covered by foreskin.
T.—One of testicles: Glands producing spermatozoa.
Sc.—Scrotum: Elastic bag containing testicles.
*V.D.—One of two tubes (Vasa Deferentia) through which sperms pass
    from testicles to the ampulla where they are stored.*
S.V.—Seminal Vesicle.
Am.—Ampulla, storehouse for spermatozoa.
Pr.—Prostate Gland that produces bulk of seminal fluid.
Bl.—Bladder.
Uth.—Urethra. Tube through which seminal fluid passes.
*Sp.—Spermatozoa: Active and free moving bodies in seminal fluid.
    Very highly magnified.*
Sm.—Symphysis or pubic bone.

microscopic bodies in the seminal fluid that is ejaculated into the vagina by the penis at the time of the male orgasm at the climax of intercourse. There are millions of these spermatozoa deposited in the vagina with each emission. They are shaped very much like tadpoles (as illustrated on page 37), and the long tail that each possesses is very active, the tail by its movements propelling the organism forward. If any of the spermatozoa succeed in entering the uterus and in making their way up the Fallopian tubes, and if one of them (it is never more than one) comes in contact with and penetrates an egg while on its journey down the tube, then pregnancy occurs.

The bulk of the seminal fluid consists of the product of glands other than the testicles, the most important of which is the prostate gland, at the base of the bladder. The main purpose of this prostatic secretion is to activate the sperms and to carry them along in the greater quantity of its own bulk. The amount of the ejaculate (the seminal fluid ejected by the male) varies of course with different individuals, and with the same individual at different times, but it is generally one-half to one teaspoonful.

At the age of puberty in a boy, the seminal fluid begins to be secreted and as full maturity is reached, the amount that is produced is usually greater than can be absorbed by the system or stored in the reservoir that is provided for spermatozoa in the neighborhood of the base of the bladder. Nature may, and does, overcome the tension induced by this accumulation by causing what are called "wet dreams" in which the seminal fluid is discharged during sleep. These experiences are sometimes disturbing to sensitive boys who have not been informed what to be prepared for. There is nothing to worry about however as it is all perfectly natural unless the experiences occur more frequently than every few days, in which case a doctor should be consulted.

Chapter IV

WHERE BABIES COME FROM

YOU probably know that in the higher animal world life is always developed from an egg that is produced in the body of the female. When a girl-child is born, its body already contains several thousand eggs of which only three or four hundred at most will ever come to maturity. These eggs, or ova, are stored in what are called the ovaries, of which there are two— one on the right side and one on the left—a short distance from the top of the uterus. (Study the diagram on page 33. The ovaries are not shown in the illustration on page 31, their position being difficult to indicate.)

When a girl matures, as she usually does anywhere from her twelfth to her fifteenth year, these eggs in her ovaries begin to mature. One of them comes to maturity every twenty-eight days, or thereabout, and is then liberated from the ovary and immediately proceeds on a journey down one of the Fallopian tubes to the uterus or womb. As soon as it begins this journey, which takes about three days to complete, the uterus begins to prepare itself for its expected guest by creating a suitable bed in which the egg may live and develop into a baby, which will happen during the following nine months provided it has been impregnated on its passage down from the ovary. This impregnation can take place only if, while on its journey down, it happens to come in contact with a spermatozoon that has been deposited in the woman's body by the male during intercourse. If this happens, the impregnated egg passes on down into the uterus, and there, in the warm moist bed that nature has provided, develops into a baby. As soon as this development is complete (in about 280 days), it has no more need of the protection of the uterus, the muscles of which begin to contract; and the baby is forced out into the world to the conscious and loving care of its mother.

If it should happen that the egg after being liberated from the ovary does *not* come in contact with a spermatozoon it dies very quickly. The uterus, however, has made provision to entertain a live visitor and can do nothing with a dead one; consequently it proceeds to get rid of the bed it has prepared. This ridding, or discarding, process takes place every month with every healthy girl after she matures, unless, of course, pregnancy has occurred. It is called menstruation.

Chapter V

INTERCOURSE AND ITS FREQUENCY

SEXUAL intercourse, coitus, coition, the sexual embrace, as it is variously called, is the entrance of the enlarged male organ into the vagina. Stimulation from this contact increases as a rhythmical in-and-out motion takes place, which ultimately produces a climax, or orgasm, for both lovers. In the man this climax accompanies the forcible ejaculation of his seminal fluid into the vagina. The focal center of the intense physical pleasure that he experiences is the glans or head of the penis, but the whole body seems to be involved in a spasm of joy that it is quite impossible to describe. For the woman the orgasm, centering in her clitoris, seems to involve every nerve in her body, and it may, and should, amount to such an intense feeling of pleasure that she may at times cry out in her ecstasy.

Sexual intercourse thus engaged in is the most intense physical pleasure of all human experience, and ought always to be just as intense for the woman as for the man. Experienced lovers will always contrive that the climax shall occur for both simultaneously. This is the ideal and it ought to be striven for. If it does not occur simultaneously, then it *must* occur for the woman first, for in that case the man will still be able to continue until his own climax is reached. But if, through precipitancy, or indifference, or inability to control himself, the man arrives at his climax first, then the penis loses its stiffness and size; and, for the time being, he is incapacitated for further intercourse; and, consequently, the climax that his wife needs to reduce the tumescence (swelling) of her sex organs, and to relieve the tension of her stimulated and expectant nerves, fails to take place—unless some expedient be adopted as will be explained a little later on.

The intelligent control of sexual intercourse, so that each time it is engaged in, it may continue for a long enough time to ensure the utmost physical pleasure and satisfaction for the wife, as well as the husband, is an art that has to be learned. Simple biological instinct, which may begin and end the whole thing in a minute, is not enough. The true lover finds other things in sexual intercourse besides the satisfaction of his own physical needs. He seeks his own satisfaction, of course, for the urge is imperative; but he seeks it from the body of the woman he loves, and while his own physical pleasure rises to the heights, he enjoys a deep mental and emotional satisfaction from the knowledge that he is the creator of an ecstatic experience for her. This feeling will of course be mutual with true lovers. Something of the technique by which the mountain-tops of sexual joy

43

may be achieved is suggested in the chapter on "The Love-Play."

One of the questions most frequently asked by young married couples is, "How often can intercourse be indulged in with due regard to health?" It is a very sensible question. The desires of the body are to be satisfied (they exist only to be satisfied) but it is wise to have reasonable concern for the future. The sexual powers on which so much of the happiness of life depends, and which should last throughout life, will be healthily maintained by their due exercise but they may be weakened by repeated excesses. No definite answer can be given to the question as to what constitutes excess and what is moderation. What may be extreme moderation for one couple may be excess for another, and what would be excess in one case may be quite inadequate for normal sex life in another. It is just a matter of sexual desire in the woman and of virility in the man, and these factors vary in every couple. Medical records tell of cases where intercourse has been engaged in as often as three times a day over very considerable periods of time. Where such a very extraordinary sex life has its source in the desires of the wife (and some women are very passionate) it would require a man to be most unusually endowed to be able to live up to her requirements for any length of time. On the other hand excessive demands on the part of the man might deplete an ordinary woman, and might result ultimately in arousing her antipathy; and that would mean disaster to home happiness.

At the other extreme there are some couples who get along when intercourse takes place only at long intervals—a month, six months, a couple of years. Such infrequency is much more apt to be due to lack of virility in the man than to lack of desire on the part of the wife. Doctor Marie Stopes, in her book "Enduring Passion," estimates that thirty per cent of married women suffer in their sex lives from lack of virility in their husbands.

Where normal sex power exists in a couple the question of frequency is simply a matter of desire coupled with an intelligent appreciation of the wisdom of moderation. In the early days of married life the act will probably be engaged in very frequently—four or five times a week or oftener; perhaps even daily for a while. It would however be unwise to keep that up very long. Generally three times, or (still better, perhaps) twice a week may in the long run be found most conducive to health and happiness. If, the day after the act, there is noticed a lack of tone in the whole system, or if any sense of weakness is experienced, it may be well to be careful. But it is unwise to be on the nervous lookout for symptoms. They are not at all likely to occur if common sense is observed. As a matter of fact, the perfectly satisfactory sex act, when not engaged in too frequently, induces a fine sense of health and strength and exaltation.

As the years go on, some change will of course take place. The ardent vigor of youth is not to be expected in a man of sixty: but where sexual infection (disease) has not been suffered from, and where common sense care has been taken of health, and where repeated excesses have not been indulged in, the sexual powers will not be unduly impaired, and intercourse satisfactory to both lovers may continue throughout life. This is the ideal in the sexual life.

A most important side of this problem however is involved in the question, How will a husband and wife get along when one wants intercourse, say every other day, while the other may feel perfectly satisfied once a week, or even less frequently? A marked difference in sexual inclinations often lies at the root of marital disharmony. Where the difference is very pronounced it may be a part of the problem of "The Frigid Wife," a subject dealt with further on under that heading. But very much of this kind of trouble in the past has lain, unquestionably, in the fear the wife may have had of becoming pregnant at a time when she did not feel equal to the task. That fear is so pronounced in some cases (and understandably so), that the wife instinctively fights shy of intercourse all the time. And where such fear exists, who can blame her?

There is a letter before me from a woman thirty-five years of age. She has eight living children and three dead. She writes from the hospital where she has been for the past three months since her last confinement.

The farm has produced no crop for five years, due to drought, and the family is on relief. She doesn't want any more children, she states, but her husband is strong and healthy, and she knows she will be pregnant within a month or two after returning home. She says she loves her husband, but is afraid that her fear of pregnancy may build up a barrier between them. She asks for birth-control information. It is manifest that satisfactory birth-control practice is the solution of very many such cases. *Take away all fear, and leave a wife free to accept the approach and stimulation of an informed husband whom she loves, and much of the difference in sex desires that we have been speaking about will disappear.*

Chapter VI

PREGNANCY

EVERY normal woman has the maternal instinct. As a girl she loved her dolls, and as a woman she wants to be a mother. She can never know the true meaning of the word "home" until, along with herself and her husband, the roof of the place they call "home" shelters the child that has come to her as the result of her love. A poet who knows something of true values has written:

> ....*a greater joy*
> *Was added, for our mutual love*
> *Had brought to us a little boy.*
> *All worldly wealth had passed us by,*
> *And yet we felt that fortune smiled,*
> *For no home knows a greater joy*
> *Than laughter of a little child.*

Pregnancy however should not occur too soon after marriage. Young couples generally look forward to marriage as a period of at least some little romance, and as far as possible it ought to be just that. But if pregnancy occurs immediately with its physical and emotional disturbances—nausea, vomiting, and probably a considerable amount of irritability in the sick wife, romance gets quite a setback. Pronounced disharmony is apt to arise. So it is generally wise to let, say, a couple of years go by before undertaking the raising of a family—a couple of years during which love and companionship and sympathies have been developed and cultivated, and mutual understanding of each other widened and deepened.

But on the other hand pregnancy should not be delayed too long. Have your children while you are young, for the nearer you are to their age the better fitted you will be to be pals together later on. And don't confine yourself to one child. It is a real misfortune for a child to be an only one. Children need brothers and sisters with whom they can play and fight and share their toys and joys and laughter and tears. They grow up healthier, less spoiled, less selfish and consequently make better men and women. Four children make a good family, if you can take care of them. If not, you should strive to have at least two.

Pregnancy is indicated by the cessation of the monthly flow, and a little later, by a slight swelling and tenderness of the breasts as dormant glands begin to function. This book does not presume to discuss matters that lie wholly within the province of the medical adviser, so there is little more to be said on this point. Just as soon as pregnancy is suspected it is well to consult an experienced physician to let him, or her, see that conditions are all right, and to get such instructions as may be considered necessary. It is best for the wife that her first pregnancy should take place before her thirtieth year.

Sometimes a wife's life is saddened because she does not become a mother. This may not be any indication of permanent sterility but just some simple matter that a medical adviser may be able to set right. It is generally recognized that a woman is most likely to become pregnant during the period from the 10th day to the 18th day of her monthly cycle counting from the first day of her menstrual flow.

INTERCOURSE DURING PREGNANCY

When pregnancy occurs there invariably arises the question as to whether, during this condition, it is right for intercourse to take place. Some people argue that it is wrong, and in support of their view they bring forward the fact that the lower animals, guided by their instinct, never copulate after the female has become pregnant. It is quite true that the lower animals do not, but men and women are in a totally different category from the lower animals. Men and women are endowed with reason and intelligence, as the lower animals are not, and their intelligence tells them that if, during pregnancy, they both want the joy of intercourse with one another, then, if it is going to do no harm, there is no reason why they should not enjoy it. And those who have made a proper study of the matter agree that no harm will be done if ordinary intelligent care is exercised. The probabilities are that it will be a positive benefit to the wife, because if, as is assumed, it is a mutual satisfaction, it will help her emotionally at a time when she needs a light heart and spirit.

Increased care must of course be taken towards the later months of pregnancy, and *during the last six or eight weeks there ought to be no intercourse at all* as it might tend to bring on premature labor. The husband at all times must be careful not to bear heavily on his wife's body. If he exercises due care the usual position for intercourse may be employed during the first two or three months. After that the side by side position will be found safest and best. Several different positions will be described under another heading.

Incidentally, we may at this point bring forward another argument that shows a radical difference between human beings and the lower animals. After conception has taken place in the animal world the female does not come to "heat" again until after she has given birth to her progeny. Among human beings, however, very many women find themselves more sexually passionate during pregnancy than before. In some cases this may be accounted for by the fear of pregnancy having previously inhibited them and caused them to repress their urge; whereas, pregnancy having been accepted, there is no further need for repression, and they can give full rein to their inclinations and desires.

On the other hand, however, there are some women

who do not desire intercourse during pregnancy. It should not be necessary to say that no sympathetic and considerate husband will ever insist on it under such circumstances. If, in spite of his loving caresses, his wife does not come to the point where she desires it, then in love and sympathy he ought to refrain from any further suggestion of it at that time. But there is another angle to this that must not be overlooked. Sympathy and loving understanding are not qualities to be manifested by husbands only. They are an integral part of the nature of every true wife, and possessing them, she will never overlook the fact that she has at all times the power to bestow her manual caresses and relieve her husband by using her hand. During the last two or three months of pregnancy this expedient may well be remembered, as at other times when intercourse may not be desirable. A man whose business keeps him away from home much of the time, returns, say for a couple of days, and his visit happens to be right in the middle of his wife's menstrual period. They may prefer not to have intercourse under such circumstances, but a real wife may well take the initiative and by means of her hand afford him the relief that he may need, and that may remove a possible temptation to him to seek for it elsewhere. By such a manifestation of sympathy and love she will certainly endear herself more than ever to her husband.

INTERCOURSE AFTER THE MENOPAUSE

Nature deprives a woman of the power to bear children after her change of life, or menopause; so if the bearing of children were the only reason for the existence of sexual passion we may be sure that Nature in her wisdom would take away that passion as soon as there would be no more use for its existence. But such is very far from being the case. A normal, healthy woman is quite likely to be subject to as intense sexual passion after fifty as she ever was. Sometimes her desires may be much more pronounced, but that again may be primarily due to the fact that all anxiety and fear about pregnancy have disappeared, and that it is possible for her to abandon herself to the joy of her husband's embrace. Her life after the menopause may therefore be just as full of love as ever it was; and if her health be good, she may enjoy intercourse as long as she lives.

It must be concluded from all this that sexual intercourse fulfils some other function in the economy of nature besides the begetting of children. Fortunately all the churches, not excluding the Roman Catholic Church, seem to have come around to this common sense view. During the past few years, in their conventions and convocations, and literature, they have been voicing the truth that sexual intercourse is not for the purpose of procreation only, but that it has a distinct value of its own as the supreme caress of married love.

As such, its exercise is not restricted to the years when a woman is able to bear children, but its blessings and joys may accompany her and her husband to relieve the grayness of life to the end.

Chapter VII

DANGERS OF ABORTION

THERE are few wives who have not at some time or other of their married lives become pregnant against their wish, and as a result been tempted to do something to themselves, or have something done, to relieve them of the undesired condition. In countries where abortion is illegal it is a cause of very high mortality. Dr. Taussig of Washington University estimates that at least 8,100 deaths occur from abortions in the United States every year. In addition to the deaths, it is very certain that tens of thousands of women are seriously injured by the operation—some of them permanently. Since, with some exceptions, performance of an abortion is illegal, it is impossible to estimate with any exactitude the number of abortions that really occur. In addition to those brought about by illegal practitioners, there are doubtless hundreds of thousands of cases where women in their desperation bring about, or try to bring about, their own abortion—often by the crudest possible means. If at any time in a married life there is good medical reason to object to a further pregnancy, the only rational thing to do is to practice birth control. The only other course open to a woman is to refrain entirely from sexual intercourse, an alternative which is very likely to wreck the home, as it will certainly wreck its happiness. But *do not interfere with your own body nor let anyone else illegally interfere with it*—it is a dangerous practice and the deaths that occur through illegal operations are painful deaths.

And one must be warned against patent medicines and drugs for "delayed menstruation," the advertisements of which are found in many magazines and papers. Insofar as they are intended to end unwanted pregnancies they are illegal, and in addition to being illegal, they are expensive, for the manufacturers are out to make money, and they know that a woman in her desperation will make almost any sacrifice in order to find relief. But after the financial sacrifice has been made, in nine cases out of ten no effects are produced; while in the tenth case a medicine strong enough to produce results will probably be strong enough to do harm.

Abortions however are sometimes necessary. There are certain conditions under which it would be fatal for a woman to become pregnant and go through with it. When two doctors in conference judge this to be the case in any particular instance, it is then perfectly legal for them to bring about what is called a therapeutic abortion—an operation that involves practically no risk when performed early by a competent surgeon. There are many cases where such interference is fully justified. Mr. Harold Chapple, Senior Gynecologist of Guy's Hospital, London, England, writes:

"For a woman with an uncompensated heart, with a family, say, of three children, to become pregnant again, is a real tragedy." Then there are certain kidney diseases which may result in convulsions and death at childbirth. Again it is asserted by authorities that out of every seven women who are afflicted with tuberculosis, four of them die, not from tuberculosis, but from childbirth. I mention all this to show the necessity of a woman being intelligently informed as to her physical condition; and that can be accomplished only by keeping in touch with the family physician. Needless to say, it is infinitely better to avoid pregnancy by birth control than to have to interrupt it in order to save the mother's life.

Chapter VIII

BIRTH CONTROL

ONE of the most pathetic things in the world is ignorance of birth-control methods by women who need the knowledge. Every moment of the day and night, the desperate cry of millions of sick and suffering mothers is going up for some knowledge that will save them from having to bring into the world more children than they can happily and adequately take care of. Hundreds of thousands of mothers the world over die yearly in agony because of the disastrous results of their desperate efforts to bring about miscarriages or abortions on themselves, or through the ignorance or carelessness of illegal abortionists. Hundreds of thousands of women die because of their physical unfitness for child-bearing. Hundreds of thousands of divorces and separations take place, and homes and lives are wrecked because of marital unhappiness arising out of the refusal by wives, through fear of pregnancy, of all sexual life to their husbands. Such conditions as these ought not to exist.

The knowledge and practice of birth control is the only practical solution of much of this misery, sorrow, pain and death. It is surely a fundamental principle of any decent civilization that every wife shall be the mistress of her own body, and possess the right to determine when she shall, or shall not, become a mother. Adequate understanding of birth control is the right of every married woman.

A normal, healthy girl who is sexually alive, and who is married at, say, eighteen years of age, has about twenty-seven years of child-bearing before her. She may very easily become pregnant every eighteen months and so would eventually have a family of twenty, or more. There are few women today who would venture on marriage at all if they knew positively they would be doomed to such a life. Fortunately they need not be so doomed. Birth control is their salvation. Outside of birth control, with its freedom from fear and anxiety, there are just the two alternatives—to accept pregnancies with or without rebellion, as often as they occur, or else to refrain from intercourse, which will in all probability mean a very unhappy and possibly disrupted home. The average man will seek elsewhere what he feels is his right in life—the satisfaction of a biologic urge, the existence and insistence of which, manifesting itself in the emotional and spiritual desire for companionship and love, was his main reason for getting married.

It is this last attempted solution that produces more divorces and separations than any other one thing. The judges of our divorce courts, and domestic relations courts, tell us that a large majority of the marital failures that come before them arise, in the first instance, out of some sexual disharmony. We can therefore put down an adequate knowledge of birth control as an absolute essential for the successful married life. The possession of such knowledge does not mean that homes are going to be childless—the maternal and paternal instincts are too strong for that. All it means is the intelligent control of pregnancies so that babies shall be spaced properly and come when they are wanted, and not otherwise. It is surely a child's right that it be born into a home where it is wanted, and into conditions of love and sufficiency where it may be properly taken care of, properly fed and clothed, and later given a fair chance to receive an education that will fit it reasonably for the responsibilities of life. Such conditions will mean healthier and happier parents, healthier and happier children, and brighter homes.

This is the view that has rapidly gained ground in recent years among all the religious bodies. Most of the important churches are now committed to the view that sexual intercourse between husbands and wives has a meaning and value of its own, as a caress and manifestation of love, entirely apart from the procreation of children, which can be guarded against when necessary by the intelligent use of harmless contraceptives.

I doubt if in the history of the world there has ever been a matter of such universal importance and interest in which all the religious authorities have been ranged on the negative side, and where, within a period of five or six years, there has been so complete a right-about-face as there has been on this matter of birth control. A few years ago all the churches maintained (at least tacitly) that the sexual functions had one object only— the begetting of children. They failed to see that such a theory puts men and women in the category of the lower animals that know nothing of the deep mental and emotional joy, the unselfish love and devotion, that may lie at the root of the perfect sexual experience.

This deeper and truer conception of sex that is now supported by the main churches of Christendom, should open the eyes of the many mothers who, from a supposedly religious motive, refuse to practice birth control. Many such mothers will acknowledge that they very certainly *do not want any more* children, and that with each child their health grows poorer and poorer, but they refuse to do anything to stop them coming on the theory that "God sends them." It is a pathetic situation. Such mothers ought to see that to bring into the world more children than they can properly take care of is doing a distinctly irreligious and wrong thing —wrong to the children who have to suffer, wrong to themselves and to their husbands, wrong to the other children, and wrong to society, which, in all probability (as things are today) may ultimately have to provide for them. Such women, if they would but reason about it, would surely see that no good "God" could possibly want all this wrong to be done in His world. In order that it may be avoided as far as possible, He has given us intelligence to devise contraceptives, and we may be sure He expects us to use them. There are many different contraceptives and, while some of them are not to be recommended, the best, if intelligently and consistently used are very effective—probably 99 per cent safe.

Birth control is almost universal among educated and intelligent people. It is impossible to avoid the fear that in many cases selfishness, and the desire to enjoy the pleasures of married life without the acceptance of its responsibilities, are at the root of the practice. Couples of reasonably good health and sufficient means ought not to be childless, nor should they be content with one or two children. The actuaries who are able to compute such matters tell us that an average of almost four children to the family is necessary to maintain a population at any given level. The average family however of the educated and intelligent people is not even three children. As the population, in spite of this, is still growing, it is manifest that we are dependent for this growth on the classes that do not practice birth control. These classes, unfortunately (outside of those who, though educated and intelligent, are governed by ecclesiastical decrees), may be called, generally, the less educated and the irresponsible, including the weak-minded. This is really a serious condition which we may hope will rectify itself when economic and international conditions take a more favorable turn.

Intelligent parents with a sense of their responsibility

towards any children they may bring into the world know that to bring up a child and educate it for any professional career means an outlay of several thousand dollars, and there are relatively few parents so financially situated that they can look on a proposition of that kind with equanimity. They know, moreover, that even with a university education a young person's future is not necessarily assured. Thousands of graduates during economic depressions were unemployed or were compelled to turn to unskilled work at low wages. When our society shall have evolved to the point where parents are freed from the fear that more children may mean more distress and poverty, we are likely to find the birth rate among our best citizens increasing. Birth control does not mean race suicide. In Holland, where birth control has been taught and practiced for some fifty years, we find not only a satisfactory birth rate, but a general improvement in the physical as well as in the mental and moral development of the people.

The mathematical consideration of population pressure is interesting and important. This earth has a fixed area which cannot be increased. But all living organisms have the inherent power to keep on increasing without end. One female codfish, for instance, spawns 2,000,000 eggs a year. If all came to maturity, and the same thing continued for only five years, all the oceans of the world would be packed tight with codfish, and every continent flooded with the displaced water. Nature, however, has birth-control methods of her own.

Dean Inge, writing in the *Pictorial Review* of March, 1932, said, "It is impossible to discuss the problem of birth control intelligently unless it is realized to start with, that in normal circumstances some method of restricting numbers is absolutely necessary." As the human race can, and would, double every twenty years if there were no restrictive influences, it is clear that in 100 years there would be a population of four billion people in the United States—twice as many as the world population today. Canada would have 320,000,000. Famine, war, pestilence, high infant mortality, abortion and infanticide have been the restrictive influences in the past. We are coming now into the age of intelligent birth control.

Chapter IX

Long Engagements Versus Early Marriages

THIS whole question is a very great problem. Children mean expense, and in these days more than ever in the past, economic conditions are such that young engaged couples are often deterred from marriage, sometimes for years, because they do not feel justified in starting in to raise a family for which they know they are not able to provide adequately.

In such cases there are three courses open. They can continue their engagement until they are in better circumstances. This may mean a matter of long years of waiting. Delays of this kind, moreover, are unwholesome, for they mean physical repression and continence at a time of life when the sexual urge is strongest. If the lovers are much in each other's company they will be subject just as frequently to a stimulation which, being unrelieved, may ultimately cause psychological and physical reactions that will be harmful. This difficulty may be solved (and of course often is) by sexual intimacies or premarital intercourse. However, such a solution, aside from being open to other very serious objections, may, unless great care is exercised, end in a pregnancy. This in turn may precipitate marriage and necessitate the immediate acceptance of responsibilities for which no provision has been made. Another solution, infinitely worse, is recourse on the part of the man to prostitutes. This may mean disease that might have not only a life-long effect on himself, but might later be transmitted to his wife and children with disastrous results.

The only rational solution, wherever it is at all possible, is to get married as soon as a home, no matter how simple, can be provided, and then to practice birth control until such time as conditions justify an addition to the family. In these days most girls of marriageable age are doing something towards their own support, and this arrangement may well continue. The pooled earnings of man and wife may suffice to keep their modest home going, and provide a reserve against the time when they are ready to assume the larger responsibility of parenthood.

Chapter X

PERSONAL HYGIENE

PERSONAL hygiene is a matter of prime importance in the married life. Many a marriage that might have been happy and successful has been wrecked on the rock of carelessness about, and indifference to, personal hygiene. Cleanliness and scrupulous care of the body are imperative. The esthetic sense should never be shocked.

A complete body-bath is not a daily necessity at all except in extreme cases. Bathroom conveniences are not found in every home and there is no sense in making a fetish out of bathing and so increasing the burdens of the day. But the daily careful bathing of the hips and thighs and sex organs should never be omitted—also the armpits; and in some cases it will be wise to wash the feet. Of course some bodies perspire more than others, and, in some, the body odor is not always agreeable. In such cases daily bathing may be compulsory. There are soaps and other preparations on the market that help to control unpleasantness of this kind, and your druggist will help you to a selection if necessary.

Then there is the matter of mouth cleanliness. Most of the time your sexual embrace will be engaged in while lying face to face. It will not be an ideal experience unless there is sweetness of breath on the part of both. The care of your teeth helps to ensure this. Particles of food get between the teeth and lodge there, and, unless removed, they decay and make the breath unpleasant. The use of dental floss by which these particles can be removed, followed by careful use of a soft toothbrush, will keep your mouth clean and help to keep the breath sweet. Tooth decay is often the cause of unpleasant breath and if it exists one should see one's dentist before it is too late. A beautiful set of teeth is a very great adornment, and everyone fortunate enough to possess one should do his or her best to preserve it. An unpleasant breath may, of course, arise from a disordered stomach, poor digestion or faulty elimination. At least one quite free movement of the bowels should be the daily rule. If there is difficulty of any kind, a doctor ought to be consulted.

Then there is the care of the hands. Clean, smooth, and carefully kept hands are a great embellishment to both men and women. Accordingly, do not neglect to give attention to your hands. Keep your nails carefully and closely trimmed. There are many men who are repelled to the point of disgust, and who would be rendered temporarily impotent sexually, by the sight of long nails on a woman, no matter how carefully they might be manicured. The thought of caresses from such a hand is not pleasant. There is an unavoidable suggestion of something of an animal with talons or claws. An equally disgusting thing to many men is the deep coloring of the nails that some women are allowing themselves to affect—why, some evil deity alone knows. Nails so colored suggest things that are not pleasant.

On the nights when sexual joys are expected, it is wise to be careful of personal appearance. A woman who has long hair has always something to do to it before retiring, and her appearance afterwards is not usually such as she would choose to have it were she about to have a photograph taken or compete in a beauty show. She should avoid all this on the nights when she expects to be in her husband's embrace and should see to it that she is as attractive as possible. Romance is something to cherish, but it is apt to fade quickly in an atmosphere of carelessness and indifference.

A special point in regard to male hygiene is here necessary. When the foreskin, or prepuce, of the penis is completely drawn back it reveals the depression which extends around the head of the penis where it enlarges from the body of the organ. This depression is normally covered by the foreskin and it retains an accumulation that should be carefully removed in the daily bath with soap and water. This procedure should be made a part of the daily toilet without fail.

Chapter XI

THE LOVE-PLAY

IN STARTING to describe some of the elements of the love-play it is necessary to make a few preliminary remarks.

(1) The practice of the love-play as a part of the normal impulse of sex is a practice far older than any form of civilization. It is observed in some form or other in all the higher forms of life—very pronouncedly among the birds. It is the legitimate prelude to any act of intercourse, and for some couples it is an absolute necessity if the married life is to have any chance of being successful and happy. Hence its importance.

(2) We must understand that *two lovers in the seclusion of their private room are a law unto themselves.* There is just one adage that Mother Nature, seconded by common sense, will always be whispering into the ears of both, and that must be their guide: *"Thou shalt do whatsoever is pleasurable to thy mate and to thyself, provided it be not harmful to either."* This assumes that both are normal beings and that there are no in-

hibitions or repressions, due to some faulty education, to be overcome.

Let us look for a moment at an analogous case. If a person sits down to a well cooked meal of excellent food served exquisitely, and then refuses to take, say, potatoes and bread and rice, because of having heard that starch has to be guarded against; and, under protest, eats a mere fragment of the fragrant and succulent roast because he once read as a child that we ought not to eat flesh; and hesitates at a cup of coffee because it is said to contain caffeine, though he has not the remotest idea what caffeine is; and refuses a glass of wine because he knows some people are drunkards; that person will neither enjoy the meal nor find it wholesome. If his health is good to begin with it won't be so very long. Other things being equal, the more that food is enjoyed the more wholesome it is. Inhibitions and repressions about this article of diet and that article of diet are fatal to happiness and health. And inhibitions and repressions are just as fatal to married love.

Indeed, as I shall explain elsewhere, a wife's repressive attitude may, for the time being, utterly destroy her husband's ability to have intercourse with her. That, of course, may suit her if her actions and attitude have been premeditated, but she can rest assured that sooner or later she will have to pay a heavy price for her unnatural indifference. When a man marries a wife he does so under the impression that he is marrying a companion, a mate, a woman of normal flesh and blood.

If he finds, time after time, that every natural impulse to which he yields is checked, he is very apt, sooner or later, to seek elsewhere for those manifestations of life and love that were promised to him at the altar and which he feels he has a right to expect. Such an attitude on the part of a wife will ultimately bring psychical disturbance to any normal man, for it makes him feel progressively more and more of a fool every time he willingly forgets past experiences and hopefully tries again, only to find himself once more cast down into the valley of disappointment and depression.

Lovers who enter their room with the slightest unnaturally inhibitory or repressive attitude, whether it spring from a faulty upbringing in the home or from a later false religious teaching, or from an out-of-place bashfulness, are endangering the happiness and success of their married life. Any repression (which will always be interpreted as a rebuke), where joyous cooperation ought to be in evidence, acts unfavorably on a more natural mate. Remember that sex, with all its mental and emotional and spiritual delights, is the gift of God, and it is essentially pure and natural. *Abnormal repression is a positive sin against nature.* Sweet abandon is the watchword that alone will let the would-be worshipers in the temple of love enter the innermost chamber and holy-of-holies of sexual delight. As one writer has said, "It is well for the man to keep his head, for he has a definite duty to perform—the most delightful duty of life—to give his mate the utmost thrill of which

72

her physical and emotional being is capable—*but his wife may well lose hers."* There is an old Italian saying that goes something like this—"A good wife is an angel in the street, a saint in the church, a living picture as she stands framed in the window awaiting her husband's return, a careful housekeeper—and an enthusiast in bed." Needless to say I am not suggesting that a wife should attempt to overwhelm her husband with sexual activities the first night. With a faulty education and as little sophistication as very many young men have, she might half scare him to death. But I do assert very emphatically that *a wife's part is never a passive one—not even on the wedding night.* The intelligent wife, understanding the significance of sex and its vital importance in the cosmic scheme of things, will be fully cooperative and will constantly be taking the initiative.

(3) A point to which very definite attention needs to be drawn is that while this is a guide-book to a successful sex life, it is not for a moment suggested that successful marriage is to be achieved by following some cut-and-dried formula or modus operandi. Fundamentally, successful marriage is a thing of *romance,* and romance is essentially spontaneous, not something attained by adhering to a set of rules. The function of this book is to give, by way of suggestion, an insight into the possibilities of marriage, that mistakes may be avoided, the common repressions and inhibitions removed, and the field left open for romance to develop freely and come to its highest. Married couples must

create their own technique. If it is inadequate, or a faulty one, the result of ignorance or selfishness, the marriage will be unsatisfactory, and in all probability will end, sooner or later, in disaster. If it is a fine and satisfactory one, success and happiness are more likely to be attained. The special object of this chapter is not to furnish any technique in detail, but rather to suggest the kind of atmosphere in which romantic love is most likely to come into its own.

The love-play with which we are now going to deal, entirely apart from the actual joy of it, is, for most couples, an absolute necessity for a full and satisfactory love-life. This can be fully appreciated only when it is understood that almost all women, as already stated, are slower in having their sexual desires aroused than are men; and, after they have been aroused, it takes them longer to arrive at their climax or orgasm.

This slowness on the part of women makes it easy to understand that where a husband is not well informed, or where he is thoughtless, or selfish, the sexual act, so far as his wife is concerned, may never amount to anything more than a mere passive accommodation to him. Such a life will become gradually less and less interesting to her, and it is very likely ultimately to become objectionable, or positively repulsive; and what might otherwise have been a happy and successful marriage comes to a tragic end. Moreover without adequate stimulation a woman's sex organs may lack the necessary moisture and so not be in a physical condition for intercourse. If such is the case the act itself may be one of pain to her rather than of pleasure.

As opposed to such crudity as this, ideal sexual intercourse follows a period, more or less protracted, of what is called the love-play. This love-play is the delicate and entrancing prelude to the delightful symphony it ushers in. The object of this prelude, apart from its own intrinsic and exquisite joy, is to create on the part of the wife a real desire for intercourse—a desire that may well rise to the point of a positive demand, depending on the skill of the husband as a lover. During it the husband caresses his mate in every way that appeals to her. It may be a progressive technique, every step of which should have its power and make its appeal. Words naturally come first—the expression of admiration and love—spoken over and over again with the natural intensity of an ardent lover's devotion. It is wise perhaps for the husband to begin without being in actual contact with his wife. Let her see that you can admire her from a distance and without the stimulation of any contact. Sit a couple of yards away where you can see the fine nuances of feelings that steal into her eyes as she hears your confession of love. She may have heard it a hundred times before, but, all being well, it will never tire her, and she will be glad to hear it over and over again down the years as the theme song of your lives. Don't hurry. Tell her again.

If you are real mates her eyes will tell you when she is anxious for your caresses. Her body has its distinct erogenous zones, that is, areas of sexual sensitivity. The face and mouth naturally come in for caresses first. It may be wise for the kisses at this stage of the game to be with closed lips. The wholly entrancing kiss of the open mouth with tongue to tongue belongs to a little later time. There is one all important injunction—*don't be in a hurry*. Caress the lobes of her ears and her neck. The human hand is the natural instrument of any caress —let it descend slowly and caressingly to her breasts and fondle and stroke them and kiss her nipples. The breasts and nipples in most women are very susceptible areas. You will notice them swelling up as they will at a later period when they are sucked by the baby in her arms—which is also, remember, a phase of sexual life. Gradually lower your hand to her waist. Let me emphasize—*don't hurry. You must give her imagination and anticipations time to work* as your hand steals slowly around, lower and lower, inch by inch, tantalizingly. There is no need to go into further detail. Ordinary impulses will inspire both mates, and the wife's anticipations will find their realization in the gentle caressing of her vulva and clitoris by the moistened fingers of the man she loves. Never use dry fingers; they hurt her.

Under the caresses of a true lover her body will begin to glow and her sex organs begin to swell and get wet with the pre-coital fluid, until finally, every cell of her body awakens and demands from her mate all that he can give her. Under these circumstances she should be able in the ensuing intercourse to arrive at a real climax. Until the husband has succeeded in bringing this climax to the woman he loves, he must never be satisfied with himself as a lover. It is the existence of this conscious sympathy with a mate that differentiates human sexual love in its highest manifestation from the lower animal sex life all around us. And this point is well worth dwelling on. The lower male animals perform their functions quite indifferent to any love, or to any climax that the female may or may not have. But the true human lover finds his highest joy in his wife's participation in the ecstasy that he himself always experiences. To men and women alone in all creation is it given to lie face to face during intercourse, and in their closest union to look into the depths of each other's eyes and see there the revelation of their mutual love and the joy that they mutually bestow. This in itself is sufficient answer to those who blasphemously assert that all human sex life is on a level with animal instincts, the only reason for the existence of which is the begetting of progeny. Such people are only advertising to their audiences the pathetic fact that they themselves have never risen above that level. They simply do not know what they are talking about. As man is higher in the scale of being than the rest of the animal world, so is his sex life capable of transcending theirs by virtue of sacrificial love, and sympathy, and unselfishness, of which the animals know nothing

In considering this important matter of the love-play

77

we must first realize that sex satisfaction is intended by nature to be a delightful sensuous experience—sensuous meaning an appeal to the senses. We have five senses and they are all ministered to in the ideal sex life—the sense of hearing, the sense of sight, the sense of touch, the sense of smell and the sense of taste. It is by just the same gratification of all the senses that the satisfaction of our hunger for food is best achieved. Undoubtedly we could eat blindfolded, consuming the coarsest of uncooked food in a most undesirable environment, and it would doubtless save us from starving to death, but it would not be very much of a meal from the esthetic point of view. Rather do we like to find our appetite being stimulated by the delicious smell of the well-cooked food, to hear the tinkle of the dinner bell telling us that things are ready, to see the table tastefully arranged with spotless linen and fine ware which is a positive delight to touch; and when we finally take our seats at the table, the taste of the delicious food is more delightfully satisfying because of an ideal environment in which we eat. Such meals are not only more delightful but more satisfying and wholesome. And it is the same with the sex life. The crudities of a few moments of intercourse in the dark (next door to rape if the wife has no desire) would doubtless fulfil all the requirements of the animal nature, so far as insuring pregnancy and perpetuation of the race is concerned. But surely we are something more than the animals. There is a refinement in the educated

78

and esthetic mind that is not satisfied with crudities, but which demands the accessories of a fine appreciation by all the senses of the joys that surely do exist.

But we must get on with a brief consideration of the different senses and the part they play in the love-life. And first of all comes "hearing." You may wonder for a moment how the sense of hearing can play a part in any sex experiences. It both can, and does, play a very important part. It comes in, in conversation. Those who neglect this stimulus and embellishment to the life of love, are neglecting one of the most important factors that go to make it interesting and enchanting. Human sex desires do not spring from rhythmical physical conditions that make themselves manifest at certain seasons of the year, as is the case with the lower animals. Like other emotions, human love and desire are subject to suggestion and imagination, both of which have their seat in the brain and not in the sex organs. A thought suggested, a word spoken, may cause a man's sexual organs to respond immediately, as indeed a sensitive woman's also. Erotic conversation is a perfectly legitimate and natural part of the love-life, and it will always be in evidence when there is no repression.

Every activity in life that is subject to discussion has its own appropriate language. Business has its own terminology and phraseology. The description of a sunset requires a different choice of words and phrases than a treatise on mathematics or a humorous sketch. And so love has its own language, words and terminology.

Uninhibited sexual love will not be satisfied with the cold, bare, scientific words of a medical textbook. Other words are necessary for lovers for their bodies and their functions. Usually they originate words for themselves. The names that you devise, or choose, for your own organs and their functions are your own secret words that may be spoken to one another whenever your fancies "lightly turn to thoughts of love." Speak of your bodies. Tell one another what stimulates you most. Discuss your feelings. Suggest further experiences and variations. Be spontaneous. Let Eros guide.

Then there is the sense of sight. Your lover was first attracted towards you, in all probability, by the face he saw and admired. He has wondered at your hair as he stroked it and, probably, buried his face in it. He has looked into your eyes and was glad to see there some reflection of his own feelings. It is soon going to be your opportunity to let him see your beautiful body in all its naked loveliness. Stand before him in your proud nakedness whenever you have the opportunity—he won't weary of the sight. Let him see that you want him to admire every charm that you possess; and it goes without saying that he will be enthralled when he sees your eyes rivetted on his own strong body. Do not make the fatal mistake of imagining that bashfulness means refinement. Recall the sublime picture of God's paradise that I have already referred to, "And they were both naked, the man and his wife, and were not ashamed."

There is the sense of touch which is, of course, the very essence of sex life. From time immemorial the holding of hands has been the first manifestation among lovers of the instinct to touch the object of one's love. The kiss that at first is a mere touching of the outward lips, but in its more intimate form is an actual contact of the mucous membrane of the lovers' mouths; the mutual feeling and caressing of the sexual organs; these are all manifestations of the universal desire to be in actual contact with the body of the loved mate.

Then there is the sense of smell and of taste. When a lover buries his face in his sweetheart's hair he finds a delicate scent that stimulates his imagination. When he kisses her mouth he glories in the fragrance of her breath, and when lips and tongues touch he realizes that he is actually tasting the secretions of the body that he hopes will some day be his more wholly to worship.

And here we come again to that matter of vital importance—the most careful and meticulous cleanliness of the body. I have already dealt with this in the chapter on personal hygiene, but it must be reiterated here. There are many marriages wrecked on the rock of carelessness. A daily bath may be a desirable luxury—it is not necessarily an essential; but a daily and careful bathing of the hips and thighs and sexual organs is imperative. This does not mean that a douche is necessary. It is not. Much douching is not wholesome, as it tends to remove the characteristic and natural secretions of the vagina. A couple of douches after each menstrual period may be advisable, or at any time if there is a definite reason for it. But the outside and inside of the labia and the hair that surrounds them should be washed carefully every day, particular care being taken with the folds of skin around the clitoris. The lips of a woman's sexual organs should be immaculately clean.

From all this you will see that the love-play is simply all and everything that both wish to do that ministers to your mutual pleasure. A warm temperature in the room is highly desirable so that you do not need to be bothered with many, or any, clothes. Then, in a warm room, and both entirely without inhibitions or repressions, it is up to you both to have all the exquisite experiences that nature has made it possible for you to enjoy.

I hope it goes without saying that the love-play is no one-sided game. It is a mutual play in which the uninhibited wife, of her own initiative, takes her active part. It is quite certain that a man sooner or later gets "fed up" with a wife's indifference *when he finds that her activities never occur except in response to his own suggestions and askings.*

OBJECT OF THE LOVE-PLAY

The love-play, in itself, is one of the most delightful experiences of married life, but it has a definite object that should always be achieved. Its purpose is to stir the wife up to the point of positive desire, because, until her desires are ardent, and her genital organs have begun to swell and produce the lubricating secretion which they do produce under proper stimulation, she may not be in a proper physical condition to engage in intercourse. This is seldom realized by inexperienced couples. Until the pre-coital fluid has made its appearance the vaginal lips are more or less dry, and the passage contracted; and if the husband attempts to effect entrance while this condition exists, it will be done only with difficulty, and often with severe pain to the wife. A husband should never have intercourse with his wife until he has awakened in her a positive desire for it, nor until he has made certain that the desire has produced sufficient lubrication to ensure that she is not going to suffer while he enjoys his pleasure. No real lover will allow that situation to arise. There are however some women (even some who are quite passionate) whose bodies do not produce sufficient moisture for lubrication. In such cases the lubricant has to be supplied.

INTERCOURSE AND ITS PROPER CLIMAX

Let us now suppose that the love-play has continued for as long as has been necessary to induce positive desire, a complete relaxation of the vaginal passage and sufficient lubrication to permit of entrance being effected with ease. Both are now ready for intercourse. I shall deal later with the different positions that may be adopted for intercourse, but here I must confine myself to restating, for the sake of emphasis, that the one absolutely necessary thing in married life is that the wife, provided she is physically capable of it, must have a proper, and satisfying, orgasm, just as her husband does. If she is a fully developed woman, without inhibitions or repressions, it may be just as intense an experience for her as it is for him. It is his concern so to practice the art of love that he may always bring this climax of complete satisfaction to his mate. It is her rightful heritage. If he succeeds, his marriage is therein a complete success on the physical side. Certainly, other things besides a satisfactory sex life are necessary for the making of a happy home, but it is no less certain that no matter what else may be present in the lives of a couple—health, wealth, admiration of genius, or power—if the sexual life of the partners is *unbalanced,* a successful and happy home is impossible. Intelligent appreciation of ideal marriage and its requirements, definite knowledge of a proper technique, and patient practice, are all needed if success is to be attained.

If you will turn to the illustration on page 31 you will see the clitoris which, as I have already explained, is analogous to the penis in the male. It is small, but it is the center of sensitivity in a woman. Under the stimulation of the delicate caresses of a lover it enlarges and hardens, and it is only by its continued stimulation that the average woman's climax can be produced. It is quite plain then, that at least one necessary thing is to keep this part of her organism stimulated until a climax is reached, and the only way this can be done is by keeping it in contact with something. As you look at the illustration you will see, however, that the clitoris is located at some little distance (sometimes being as much as an inch and a half) from the vaginal entrance where intercourse takes place, and without a full appreciation of this fact intercourse may *take place and end without its ever having been even touched*. With the vast majority of women this would never produce an orgasm. The trouble is just plain ignorance on the part of both. If the woman knows more about her own anatomy, which is quite likely, than her husband does, then it is up to her to inform him. The inexperienced lover has almost always the misconception that intercourse means penetration and an in-and-out motion, and nothing more.

If you will look at the illustration on page 31 and try to visualize the male organ having made a *complete* penetration, you will see that under this condition the clitoris will be in actual contact with the husband's body immediately above the base of the penis. While in that contact, a side-to-side motion of the hips, or a circular motion, by either husband or wife (to be achieved perhaps only after some little practice), will ensure the clitoris being stimulated as it could not be by an in-and-out motion only—a motion that necessarily means a repeated breaking of the contact, which should

85

be avoided as much as possible during the early part of the union.

This brings up the important matter of the duration of a period of intercourse. How long should intercourse last on each occasion? No definite answer can be given further than to say that if it is to be satisfactory it *must* continue until the wife has had a complete orgasm —provided of course that she is physically capable of having one. For most wives with normal sensitivity it ends very much too soon, as a general thing. It has to end, of necessity, as soon as the husband has had his orgasm; and with a continuous in-and-out motion a man will arrive at his climax very quickly. That of course ends the seance and the woman may find herself left "up in the air," so to speak, excited, her tumesced organs still congested and her nerves on edge; while her mental attitude toward the inefficiency of her husband would not make him conceited were he aware of it. Such a conclusion as that, time after time, would become unendurable for any normal woman, and it must be avoided if the sexual side of married life is to mean anything to her. The problem for the lovers then is first to arouse a positive desire on the part of the wife by the love and caresses of the love-play, and then to carry on intercourse for the pure enjoyment of it for as long as may be desired, and finally to be sure that it ends with a completely satisfying orgasm for the wife.

The problem resolves itself very largely into this: Assuming the husband has aroused his wife's desires,

86

how long can he carry on intercourse before ejaculation occurs? Unfortunately many men suffer from premature ejaculation—which may take place within a few seconds after penetration, and sometimes even before penetration has been effected. There are still more men whose ejaculation, while not premature, is nevertheless too soon, usually within a minute or two after penetration.

For such men several expedients may be tried. What is necessary is, of course, to lessen the sensitivity of the glans, or head of the penis. This can be done by applying a weak solution (2%) of novocaine. Five minutes after the application the surface nerves will be temporarily dulled and consequently ejaculation will be delayed. Another expedient is to wear a sheath or condom, which makes an artificial foreskin and is effective in reducing sensitivity. If the sheath is put on while the foreskin is still covering the head it will help to retain it in place, and under these conditions there will be a much greater range to the possible time for continuation of intercourse.

It must not be understood from anything that has so far been said that, just because a woman might be made to arrive at her orgasm, say in a couple of minutes, that therefore it is desirable she should do so. Very far from it. True intercourse is a time of mental and emotional, as well as physical, communion between a man and his wife, and it may well be continued for any period that is short of producing a sense of weariness or exhaustion—ten minutes, twenty minutes, half an hour or longer. Some women are able to experience more than one orgasm during a seance, though the second or third may be of less intensity than the first. This ability is not enjoyed by the man, and, when his climax has been reached, active intercourse has to cease for the time being. The climax may be delayed by refraining from much, or any, motion, until both are ready to complete the seance.

Let me caution every wife on one point. Do not get into *the habit* of pretending your passion has been aroused and that you have enjoyed an orgasm, thinking thereby to please your husband. There are occasions when, for one reason or another, it may be all right to practice a little harmless deception of that kind. You love your husband and want to please him, and it won't hurt you—*but don't make a practice of it*. You are entitled to just as much joy out of your sexual intimacies as your husband is, and it is your rightful heritage. Moreover, sooner or later he is going to suspect the fraud, perhaps by the condition of your sex organs, and the moment he does that, you may find him pause suddenly in his caresses and become lost in thought. When a husband during love-play suddenly stops and begins to think, it isn't a good sign. He is probably wondering if all the rest of your attitude towards him is camouflage too. Your body probably is capable of perfectly satisfactory stimulation if it is properly handled and caressed. If you will cast behind you all fears and repressions and inhibitions that are so fatal to proper physical responses, and will train your husband in every little love trick that your woman's wit can devise, you will not need any camouflage to make him satisfied.

Chapter XII

THE FIRST NIGHT

ONE of the main inspirations responsible for the writing of this book is knowledge, possessed by every psychiatrist and experienced physician, of the fact that in thousands of cases the chances for married happiness which seemed so bright in the morning, among the assembled friends with their flowers and gifts, are hopelessly destroyed within twenty-four hours of the performance of the marriage ceremony. Nothing could be much more tragic in life than that. Let every man be wise. The marriage night and the honeymoon may well be the beginning of life-long happiness—a happiness deepening as the years roll by—or they may end in disappointment and aversion that will be hidden perhaps by the outraged bride, but which will find vent in the bitter tears of disillusionment and disgust, and affect the balance of life.

Many a woman who might have been developed by a wise lover into a devoted and ardent wife has become frigid, and sex in all its manifestations has become repellent to her, because of psychological, and perhaps physical, shock, due to the blundering of an inconsiderately aggressive and ignorant husband. The true lover will solicitously see to it that his first intimacy with his bride shall have nothing in it to offend. Indecent haste to consummate the marriage is a sign of nothing more than indecent haste, and not of true love. A woman is practically raped if intercourse is forced on her at a time when she is not ready for it and when she does not desire it. And it does not follow that she is ready for it or desires it just because she was married a few hours ago. It is quite possible that she may be more or less bashful, and, if so, her lover needs to show understanding and sympathy and to be thoughtfully considerate to the last degree. It may well be a testing time for him, for his love and self-control. There is a heavy responsibility resting on him. First impressions and experiences are always important and he is going to make himself responsible for the first experiences and impressions of married life with the girl he has chosen to be his sexual companion for life. The first night is the first approach towards the full and perfect relationship that each hopes for, and it is a night of supreme importance—as well as of exquisite possibilities—for both.

Let the husband remember that the preceding few weeks have been a time of unusual strain on his wife. She has had things to do that he has no idea of—preparations of all kinds to make, clothes to get ready, friends to entertain, letters to write, the wedding to arrange for, all in addition to her usual duties, while he, in all likelihood, has had nothing more to do than his customary daily work. His good sense ought to tell him to go slowly and considerately. If in any way he coarsely forces himself on his wife, excited and tired though she be, to obtain what he imagines are his "rights," he will be making a blunder—quite possibly an irreparable one. I use the word "irreparable" advisedly. He must know that he is treading on dangerous ground if he "claims" anything at all that she does not feel prepared to give.

Balzac makes the wise observation, "A man should never permit himself the pleasure with his wife which he has not the skill to make her desire." That is true all through married life but especially is it true on the wedding night. The part he has to play is the part of the fine and considerate lover. If he fails, the night may not pass before the girl begins to harbor doubts as to whether or not she has made a mistake. More psychological damage may be done the first night, or during the honeymoon, than the balance of life will be able to correct. She may feel that her heart and soul as well as her body have been outraged. Of all the days and nights of married life the honeymoon may well be the most important, because during it the foundation for either future happy or unhappy sexual relationship will be laid—and foundations are not easily changed. Let every man go slowly and carefully, and every woman be sympathetic and wise.

As I have already said, this book does not pretend to lay down any cut-and-dried rules for the guidance of lovers. That would be absurd. Love must be spontaneous or it loses its romance. But the accumulated wisdom recorded in the many volumes about love that the ages have produced can at least warn us of things that should not be done, and make suggestions that may stimulate a backward imagination and so encourage spontaneity by indicating possibilities.

Naturally, personalities and conditions differ in every case. There are some things, however, that are almost invariably true. The girl, as already stated, may appear in good health and strength and yet she may be nervously tired after the days of work and excitement that have preceded the wedding. If so, she is certainly not in a condition to go through a unique experience, of which she may possibly be thinking with some little anxiety and bashfulness—perhaps some little fear. Both she and her husband will experience the utmost thrill from their first intimacy only if both are at the peak of physical fitness. This is something to think of. In most cases it will be wise to defer the consummation of their marriage for a night or two—or even longer.

But this deferring of actual union need not withhold from them some of the delights of their new relationship. If the lover-husband will take his wife on his knee, and with her head buried on his shoulder and while she is still fully dressed, gently caress her with his fingers until he brings about an orgasm (perhaps the first she has ever had), he will be introducing her to an ecstatic experience that she will certainly never forget. He will be demonstrating his own restraint for the time being, and will be manifesting a sympathy and consideration that will pay big dividends. Compare such an introduction to sexual life with the practical raping, perhaps several times in a night, of a tired and nervous girl by an inconsiderate man intent only on his own gratification. If the bride has any fear or nervousness, the procedure mentioned obviates the necessity of her undergoing experiences that may need great care and patience (an obdurate hymen for instance) if any and every form of anxiety and distress is to be avoided in an initiation that should be altogether one of joy.

Although I have touched on the matter in the chapter on the female sex organs, it is necessary to refer again at this point to the hymen, or so-called maidenhead. Let no man expect to find an intact hymen in his bride, or dare to be disappointed at not finding it, or imagine for an instant that either its presence or its absence necessarily means anything at all. The hymen is a quite variable quantity. Doctors sometimes find an unruptured hymen in a woman who is pregnant, which has to be cut before the infant can be born. In some cases a rudimentary hymen may exist even after childbirth. And on the other hand there are many virgins who were born without hymens. Sometimes too the hymen may have been ruptured accidentally in childhood; sometimes by medical treatment. It is to be hoped that

94

every girl who reads this book may be wise enough to see to it that her hymen is either nicked or stretched before her marriage. Much distress may be saved by so doing and the possession of this book will be sufficient explanation if any should ever be necessary. But no man has any right to offend his wife by even the slightest reference to the matter. It is the future that is all-important—not the past.

Chapter XIII

DIFFERENT POSITIONS FOR COITUS

THERE are different positions that can be taken in sexual intercourse and it is desirable that the position should be varied just as often as fancy may chance to dictate. Variety in sex technique, as in most other things in life (tea out in the garden, for instance), adds a certain spice that need not be refused for any reason known to common sense. Lovers should see to it that the delightful abandon of sexual love shall manifest itself in any variety of experience that mutual ingenuity cares to devise.

Entirely apart, however, from the question of choice for the sake of variety, the adoption of different positions for the sex act becomes, at times, a matter not only of physiological wisdom (for a pregnant wife's sake, for instance), but one of physical necessity, as in the case of extreme obesity.

The usual position is for the wife to lie on her back with her thighs widely separated and her knees bent, while her husband lies between her legs and supports himself on his knees and elbows, so that practically none, or very little, of his weight rests on his wife's body. This is important because she needs to be able to move herself in any way that her feelings may prompt.

The bending of her knees and the drawing up of them towards her chest is important. Many couples have found themselves unable to consummate their marriage properly because they were trying to do it with the wife lying with her legs stretched straight out. In that position the angles of the male and female organs do not coincide and penetration is almost impossible. In addition to the proper elevation of her knees, she may with advantage place a pillow under her hips, which will enable her husband to effect an entrance more easily, and herself to embrace him with her legs as she will want to do.

In this position the lovers are face to face—a position as already stated that belongs to the human race alone. Such a fact is worth thinking about. It suggests that with human lovers, sexual intercourse may be something more than a bare experience on the physical plane. The sexual mates can look into each other's eyes during the whole period and find joy in mutual endearments and caresses, and in observing the nuances of love and rapture as each contributes to the other's joy.

Then there is the side-by-side position, face to face, with the upper thigh of the wife thrown over the opposite thigh of the husband. It is a restful position and admits of each being in the embrace of the other and, if it be desired, of going to sleep while sexually united.

Again, when desired, the woman may assume the "superior" or upper position, the man lying flat on his back while the woman kneels, or squats, across him. This upper position gives the woman complete freedom to move according to her inclination, and, as it also admits of deep penetration and very close contact, it is sometimes effectual in bringing about her orgasm where other positions fail.

Sometimes the sitting position will be adopted. In it the man sits on an armless chair with the woman across him. There is no particular advantage in this position beyond the fact that it is a variation, and at times may possess an element of stimulation. We must clearly understand that there is nothing unnatural or abnormal in adopting any position at all that occurs to lovers when it affords mutual pleasure. Different positions in coitus are adopted in different places according to inherited custom, just as different customs and positions are adopted at meals. Our Western custom is to eat while seated on a chair at a table, while Eastern people prefer to sit on the floor. Few people would care to suggest that the Japanese, for instance, are less civilized than we, just because of things like that. There are certain tribes among whom the side-by-side position in coitus is considered the only correct one. They believe that the upper-and-lower position, that is most common among us, is morally wrong. It is all a matter of custom and inclination.

The only other position I shall mention is the rear, or spoon-shaped position, in which both lie on the same side, the husband facing his wife's back, with his hips extending far enough under her to allow of at least partial penetration. In this position also it is possible for them to go to sleep while in union, and it can be taken at any time when there is no desire to arrive at an orgasm. If an orgasm should be desired while in this position it may be necessary for the husband to put his arms around his wife's hips and help her to "arrive" by gently caressing her with his fingers.

This method of helping a wife to arrive at her climax is very important. As I have already stated more than once, most women are much slower than men in reaching their orgasm. It is, of course, the husband's special care that his wife shall experience all the ecstasy that her body is capable of, but it will sometimes happen that, in spite of his desire and intention, he will find it impossible to restrain his ejaculation, and his orgasm will occur while his wife is perhaps nowhere near her climax. When this happens, if no expedient be adopted, he will leave his wife disappointed, and her actual physical requirements unsatisfied, for the simple reason that he will, for the time being, have lost his ability to have any further intercourse with her. In this real emergency there is only one thing to do and that is to gently caress her clitoris and the surrounding lips with his moistened fingers until she too arrives at her orgasm.

The important thing is that if she is capable of an orgasm she *must* experience it, one way or another: her physical, mental and emotional health demand it. The skilful lover will always avoid this unequal ending. The ideal is to "arrive" simultaneously. During intercourse therefore conversations will take place and the lovers will inform each other how the game is going. If the wife is lagging, and needs a little more stimulation, her husband can put his hand down between them and caress her clitoris as intercourse continues, or she may help herself. The experience of each will guide them in all this and it should soon be possible to bring about a simultaneous arrival at the goal.

It is not my intention to go into any further detailed description of the other various positions that may be adopted in the sex act. Enough has been said to indicate that variety is possible, and, within the limits of mutual pleasure, there is nothing to prevent husband and wife from varying their procedure according to their inclinations. In the "Encyclopaedia of Sexual Knowledge," written by eminent medical men and edited by Dr. Norman Haire of London, England, eleven different positions are described. There is nothing to be gained by my going into such extended detail in this modest volume. It has been necessary, however, to indicate the possibility of variety in position, because in some cases it is compulsory. Certain physical conditions in either husband or wife, or both—obesity for instance—may make the first or common position almost a physical impossibility. And during the later months of pregnancy (*though not the last two months during which no intercourse should take place*) a different position, as is suggested in the section dealing with that matter, may be not only advisable but perhaps imperative for the wife's best welfare. Ordinary intelligence and common sense ingenuity however will always find a way to overcome any such situation provided there are no inhibitions such as may arise from a wrong mental attitude towards experiment and variety.

The sexual act, in perhaps nine cases out of ten, is followed within a moment or two by the husband's withdrawal, and the embrace ends, with perhaps an entire separation and complete insulation of the bodies of the couple. This is a mistake—a very tremendous mistake—if the husband has failed to bring his wife to a completely satisfying orgasm. She certainly won't fail to realize the quite apparent fact that the whole procedure has been nothing more than a demonstration of pure selfishness on her husband's part, and, though she may keep her feelings to herself, she will resent it. If it becomes a constant occurrence it is quite apt to wreck the home.

Assuming however that a completely satisfying climax has been reached by both, the organs should not be immediately separated. A motionless embrace should be continued for a few minutes under the influence of the deep satisfaction that each has brought to the other. Sometimes, while still maintaining their sex contact, they will choose to adjust themselves in a face to face position side by side and succumb to the sleep that so soon follows satisfactory intercourse. Detumescence will already have taken place for both, of course, but the organs are still together and they may stay that way during the first sleep.

Chapter XIV

COITUS RESERVATUS

WHAT is known as "coitus reservatus" is sexual intercourse engaged in and enjoyed as a caress without arriving at, or desiring to arrive at, any climax or orgasm. This is understood by both husband and wife from the beginning of the period, and neither of them does anything to upset this understanding. To the uninitiated, this might seem an extremely unsatisfactory sort of intercourse, but it has its place, and rather important place, in the married life. It is purely a caress and can bring just the satisfaction that is desired in that particular union. Very little love-play is necessary, in fact it is better to dispense with it entirely, as its stimulating influence might overcome the determination not to arrive at a climax. The only thing that is necessary is sufficient lubrication. The union takes place but without much, or any, subsequent motion, as that would lead up to an orgasm. Instead there is just a mutual love communion, talking, kissing, caressing, which may last for half a minute, five minutes, or half an hour. It is well for the husband to have complete penetration as there will be perhaps less tendency to any motion under that condition. As opposed to intercourse that is intended to go on to a climax, the wife may have a pillow under her head, as conversation is a little easier so.

Sexual desire varies, of course, in intensity, with the same individual at different times. If a couple have been separated for a period, it goes without saying that the desire will be more intense the first night they are together again than it will the following morning. In the morning, however, they may enjoy a few moments' caress without caring to repeat the more intense experience of the previous night. This is perhaps the time and place where the chief value of coitus reservatus lies; it is, of course, no satisfaction for very ardent desire. As against the practice it may be said that it is not certain that it would not deplete the sexual powers of a man if it were engaged in too often, or carried on too long at a time. As a brief caress it has its place, and moderation is not likely to hurt anyone. It is very certain that a man's whole outlook on life, his ambition, and his courage, are affected by his feeling of sexual ability, and, this being so, the stimulation of a few moments of coitus reservatus and *the sense of reserve power with which it leaves him*, together with the atmosphere of congenial companionship it may generate between himself and his wife, may make a good beginning for the day.

It must, however, be understood (and guarded against, if necessary) that there is a bare possibility of pregnancy occurring in spite of the fact that no orgasm is experienced by the man. Under strong stimulation a few drops of mucus is almost always observed coming from the male organ. This in itself, as mucus, could not bring about pregnancy, but at times, in some cases, it may be accompanied by a very slight escape of semen which might cause pregnancy. This escape of semen is not felt or recognized in any way by the man, and couples are occasionally astonished to find pregnancy has occurred without any apparent reason for it. The explanation may be as given above.

Chapter XV

AUTOEROTISM

MASTURBATION

WHEN people, experiencing sexual stimulation, secure satisfaction by a self-produced orgasm by means of their hands, the practice is called autoerotism, or masturbation, or self-relief. There is no doubt that it is an extremely common practice. It has been said that, in an unsigned questionnaire, probably 95 per cent of all normal men will acknowledge that they have practiced it more or less at some time of their lives, and that the five who deny having done it are probably lying. As the sex urge is generally stronger in boys than in girls, the practice is more common among them; but it is very common with girls too.

There used to be a vast amount of literature scattered about the country by unprincipled patent medicine firms that reaped a great harvest from their lying suggestions that the practice was terribly injurious, and that those guilty of it were all headed for the insane asylum—unless they stopped it and began taking the treatment advertised. Such firms are no longer allowed to advertise and operate. Ten thousand times more harm was done by their lying suggestions than by the practice itself. Commercial interests however were not the only offenders. Well-meaning, but ignorant, evangelists of one kind and another, going up and down the land, often dwelt on the matter in meetings advertised "for men only." They did infinitely more harm by the groundless fears they aroused than they did good. Doctors and psychiatrists know today that practically no harm comes from it where it has not been carried to excess, or where the sense of guilt has not been driven home. Indeed, there are very many doctors who consider that highly sexed boys and girls suffer much less harm from affording themselves occasional relief than they would suffer from attempts at repression. Understand, I am not advising a recourse to this practice as a general thing, but it is necessary to look the matter squarely in the face. Our social and economic conditions today make it practically impossible for young people to get married, as nature demands, at an early age, and under such conditions, if they are strongly sexed, self-relief may act as a safety-valve. The alternatives are either premarital intercourse with a sweetheart, which has among other great dangers the very manifest one of pregnancy; or else recourse to the exceedingly dangerous alternative of the prostitute, and, as one able woman writer has said, "better ten years of masturbation than one infection of venereal disease."

The main danger in the practice of self-relief lies in the effect of the false teaching about it—that it is a very sinful and abnormal act that is certain to induce physical and mental, and, presumably, spiritual ruin. Havelock Ellis, the great English sexologist, after wide investigation, states that in the case of moderate masturbation in ordinary healthy individuals, no injurious results will necessarily follow. Thus masturbation does not necessarily come under the head of self-abuse. Only when carried to excess could it be so termed, and any excess must be strongly deprecated. Young persons, if married, would in all probability have sexual intercourse four or five times a week, and sometimes oftener. When they are unable to get married, and they find the sexual urge to be a matter of extreme physical and emotional distress, it is not likely to hurt them if they should occasionally be forced to resort to self-relief.

The need of sane teaching in this matter is very great and its value incalculable. Every physician and psychiatrist could give many instances of the evil effect of wrong teaching. Here is one from my own experience, and it is only one of very many: A young woman wrote me in the deepest mental distress. She admitted that she had masturbated occasionally under a quite intense urge, but the act had always been followed by great remorse, because she had been taught that it was a terrible sin which God would punish by making her childless if she ever got married. As she was now about to be married, she was passing through a period of intense self-reproach. Her sense of guilt was pathetic. A couple of educative letters however cleared up the whole trouble and she was duly married and is now a happy wife and mother.

Undoubtedly the continued and excessive practice over long periods of time may ultimately result in undesirable conditions both physical and social. At the worst, where the habit has grown into actual self-abuse, it will, of course, deplete physically, though probably not more so than the same amount of abuse of the marriage relationship. If a keen sense of guilt has accompanied the act, self-reproach may build up a sense of inferiority disadvantageous to the social life. And it may unfit one for marriage. With proper education, however, of adolescent boys and girls, the practice, if they ever resort to it, will never grow into any such abuse and will cease. This is where the responsibility of parents comes in. Children should be guarded against developing any special sense of shame about their sex organs. As adolescence approaches they should be informed quite fully of the function of the organs, taught the importance of them, and their relation to the happiness of life. But very great care should be taken not to instill a fear of dread consequences of masturbation. Nine out of ten of the boys, with a little less percentage of the girls, will unquestionably experiment with themselves sooner or later. We can make up our minds to that. But every physician and psychiatrist knows that fear, and anxiety, and sense of sin, and shame, and the resultant self-reproach, do not deter from the practice when the urge becomes very insistent. Instead, these are the main cause of any bad effect that may result from the practice.

Chapter XVI

TEMPORARY IMPOTENCE

A MAN'S sexual organs and their reactions (particularly if he is of a highly temperamental type) are apt to be extremely sensitive to the attitude of his mate. Even in the presence of his sweetheart, or wife, he may be utterly oblivious to the very existence of his sex organs, and then by some touch, or word, or look, or observed position, he may immediately experience a stimulation that may make him almost instantly able for the sex act.

But it is not generally understood by women (and very often not by men until they happen to experience the phenomenon with something of dismay and resentment) that the reverse of this may occur. A man may be with his wife, his body throbbing with a desire that is all the more intense because of his belief that she is equally affected and interested, and then by some adverse thing in her attitude he may be mentally shocked and almost instantly reduced to impotence. The adverse attitude may be nothing more than some totally irrelevant remark showing that her mind is elsewhere when he had supposed that her interests were all concentrated on himself and the immediate present. A critical word, a tensed muscle (that shows an inhibition), a sigh even, may affect him unfortunately. The effect she produces is, of course, only temporary, but such experiences are to be guarded against. Men don't like them, and any wife with ordinary common sense will avoid bringing them about. In any particular instance the fault may, of course, have lain with the husband—a failure on that occasion as a lover. Had he succeeded in working up his wife to the point where her desires were as pronounced as they ought to have been, she would not have been in the least degree concerned with irrelevant matters.

Temporary impotence may also arise in the otherwise quite virile man through bashfulness, or anxiety lest he may not be able to play the part of a man. Under such circumstances a tactful wife will never let her husband see that she notices or deplores the condition. If she will suggest to him that she likes to observe the effect of her caresses, and proceeds to let him see her as she plays with his body, the impotence is likely soon to disappear.

Another possible cause of temporary impotence is fear on the part of the husband of causing pain to his partner. The remedy, manifestly, is to see to it that no pain is caused. When intercourse is attended with pain to the wife it is very often because of lack of the pre-coital fluid that lubricates the passage. But that lack is probably evidence that the wife was not sufficiently stimulated before penetration was attempted. An extension of the love-play until there is complete relaxation of the vaginal walls and a sufficiency of the pre-coital fluid, will probably right everything. If pain persists, a medical examination should be made. Sometimes wives injure their sexual organs by using too strong douches. Such things as lysol, carbolic acid, and bichloride of mercury should *never be used except under medical direction.* Irreparable harm may be done.

When a man finds that impotence at times interferes with his sexual activities, he doesn't need to worry. To start doping himself with pills of one kind and another is a mistake. Go to an experienced doctor and talk the matter out fully. Nine times out of ten there will be nothing more the matter than some slight functional disarrangement having a psychological foundation, and the talk with the doctor will be all that is necessary. *And the wise wife may be the best of all physicians.*

Chapter XVII

THE FRIGID WIFE

THERE are some women who have, apparently, very little or no sexual passion; they have no physical desire for intercourse, arrive at no climax or orgasm during intercourse, and consequently have no physical delight in the act. It is quite possible for them to become mothers and they may have many children, but the natural physical ecstasy that should be theirs is, unfortunately, totally unknown to them. Many of them realize their misfortune and would do anything if they could only enjoy what is so evidently a very great pleasure to their husbands.

On the other hand, there are some who seem destitute not only of ability to experience an orgasm, but also of any desire to do so. They seem to accept intercourse as an unavoidable part of married life, but their acceptance is in the spirit of a martyr and the act becomes at the best, a matter of indifference to them, and, at the worst, a matter of positive aversion. Certainly no home could possibly be happy under such circumstances.

This is really a very serious problem. It seems, perhaps, a mistake for any woman to get married unless she has at least some sense of a desire for sexual experiences. If she has none, then, no matter how innocent and unsophisticated a young husband may be, the time will surely come when he will realize that there is something wrong and abnormal, and disappointment and dissatisfaction may develop and another home go down in disaster.

There is hope however for such cases even as these. There is a grave doubt in the minds of many physicians and psychiatrists as to whether there is really such a thing as a positively and permanently frigid wife, provided she loves her husband *and provided he is patient and fully informed*. Her frigidity is, perhaps, nothing more than evidence that she has not, so far, experienced the special sexual stimulation that happens to be necessary in her case. In many cases the fault lies in mutual lack of knowledge—both may be totally unfamiliar with the simple facts of sex anatomy. For instance, the clitoris is the center of sexual feeling in a woman and contact with it is generally necessary for full stimulation. Its distance however from the vaginal opening differs in women, varying from half an inch to as much as an inch and a half. Where it is far from the opening it is not likely to get any stimulation from the act of coitus. Under such circumstances, an independent stimulation of it may be absolutely necessary.

Then again, the wife may lack the right mental attitude towards sex and marriage, without which no union can be satisfactory. There is no doubt that much unresponsiveness to normal sex stimulation is due, not so much to lack of sex education as to an entirely false education, due to unfortunate family influence, or wrong religious teaching, in childhood. The unwise attitude of parents towards any sex impulse in their children; punishment for simple and perfectly natural manifestations of interest in their sex organs; the sad suggestions of an association of sex with sin, and the general traditional reticence in regard to it; fears of sex through having heard of some unfortunate experience of another; these, or any one of a dozen malign influences may build up in a sensitive girl inhibitions that may make a later normal life almost impossible. The only remedy is a complete re-education that will, with sympathy and understanding, remove the barriers that keep her from her rightful heritage of being a happy wife and mother.

It is the hope of the author that this book may prove such an educative influence in those cases where it is needed—to impress the fact that sex impulse is not only right, natural and essentially pure, but that the joys attendant on it are *the rightful heritage of every woman*. If she is of a deeply religious turn of mind she can assure herself that sex is essentially religious, if obedience to natural laws constitutes any part of religion. It is the God she believes in who has given the possibilities of sexual joy to all His creatures, and she may be very sure that He expects His gifts to be appreciated, and enjoyed, and not scorned. The hope of a complete and ecstatic orgasm is hers to cherish and to strive for with all her wisdom and power. Its possession may make all the difference between a happy and an unhappy marriage. With her desire for a full experience aroused, it is then up to her husband to practice in loving patience every phase of the art of love as suggested in this book, and make it the one object of his own sexual life to bring his loved mate into her full heritage. Where there is inability to arrive at an orgasm at the beginning of married life it need not be assumed that it is a permanent or hopeless situation. Patience and time may be necessary. Normal sensitivity may not develop until after the first baby has been born. The full cycle of the sexual functions is never completed in any woman until pregnancy has been accepted and a child born. The complete sexual cycle—intercourse, pregnancy, childbirth and motherhood—may arouse the dormant sexual nerves and the outcome be perfectly satisfactory.

The girl who has occasionally practiced autoerotism (self-relief) is not likely to be in the category of the frigid wife, as is often erroneously supposed. Autoerotism presupposes the existence of at least some sexual sensitivity. The trouble with the frigid wife is that she is practically destitute of any such feeling.

Where a wife definitely deplores her lack of sexual sensitivity, and would give much to develop a natural condition in herself, it is at least possible for her to experiment and see if she can arouse some vestige of pleasurable feeling. Once that has been experienced, the goal of a perfectly satisfactory married life lies before her.

Some women are very much more apt to be sexually alive in the daytime than at night. This may be because of the drain of the day's work on their physical strength. It is a mistake to suppose that sexual joys have always to be put off until night. One primary necessity of the married life is *spontaneity*. If stimulation is experienced at noon, before there has been brought about any sense of weariness, the common sense thing is to act accordingly. Another ten or twelve hours' work may drive out completely all desire for anything but sleep.

Lack of sexual tone in some cases may be owing to some glandular inactivity. Modern medicine is alive to this problem, and has already produced extracts that are at the command of the physician. Ovarian, mammary, thyroid, pituitary or other extracts may be indicated. If necessary, see your doctor early and explain the whole situation very candidly.

In some cases intercourse terminates for a woman in a partial orgasm that promised to be pleasant at the beginning but which proves disappointing. Something seems to shut off the almost attained climax, and it is distinctly unpleasant. This may be due to some physical condition—a hooded clitoris perhaps—that can be cor-

118

rected by a trifling operation in a few minutes by a surgeon. Whenever this condition exists it should be attended to at once, as its presence makes satisfactory intercourse impossible.

Chapter XVIII

CONCERNING MANY THINGS

I HAVE now initiated you as much as I can, within the limits imposed upon me, into some of the most important facts of love, sex and marriage; and if you will read and re-read with thoughtful care, you will be fairly well equipped to set out with confidence on the sea of actual realization. Much of what I have written has been more or less by way of suggestion. As I have already said, it is for you and your chosen partner to develop your own individual technique in the matter of sex. The only absolute essential to ideal marriage on the sexual side are mutual love and admiration, with a total absence of hurtful inhibitions or repressions, and, consequently, a joyous abandonment to all the phases of normal physical love. But married life has facets, or sides, other than the purely sexual, and I must add a few pages dealing with some of these, for they are of vital importance to the happiness of the home.

As I started out by saying, ideal marriage is a life-long companionship between a man and a woman and it is founded primarily on the physical attractions of sex. Where the sex life is not satisfactory nothing in the world can possibly compensate for the lack. But on the other hand, the physical sex life may be quite satisfactory and yet the life of mental and emotional companionship that is so necessary may be totally nonexistent. Sex interest may dominate the situation for ten minutes, or half an hour, or an hour, two or three times a week; but that leaves a vast number of hours and days and weeks and months and years, in which other interests, mental, emotional, social or recreational, have to exist if there is to be any real companionship. This other section of life needs wise thought and unselfish consideration on the part of both lovers. Unless you are both prepared to consider this matter seriously, with an eye to its importance, your home can never be truly happy —or safe.

For instance, if the husband selfishly wants to bury his nose in a book evening after evening, and the wife (in retaliation perhaps) persists in letting the radio blare out all the latest jazz and senseless crooning, there is not likely to be much of the peace that passeth understanding in that home. If the wife loves art and music, while the husband has neither ability nor desire to appreciate either, she is going to feel a lack in life. On the other hand, if he is intellectually inclined and from time to time seeks to explain little things to her so that she may have at least a bare knowledge of what it is that interests him, and, without the slightest comment, she takes up again the fashion magazine she laid down when he commenced to speak, we may be pretty sure that there is going to be a "rift in the lute" sooner or later in that house. He needs someone to talk to who is sympathetic with his interests.

It is a fine thing when a wife will read to her husband, and when he will read to her, things they both enjoy. This Twentieth Century is certainly the most terrifically interesting era any human being has ever lived in, and both should try to keep in touch with world affairs, at least to some degree, so that they can discuss them together intelligently and give one another their own angles of vision. They should learn some games that two can play, so that they won't always have to be dependent on neighbors for an evening's entertainment. Friendships are, of course, to be cultivated, and agreeable neighbors are desirable, but it is a real misfortune for a couple to be constantly compelled to look outside their own home for diversion and entertainment.

To the wife especially I would say: Be careful and don't incur too many social obligations that are going to make inroads on your time and energies to the detriment of your home. You can't refuse to take some little part in the social world around you, but I assure you that "Ladies' Aids," and church committees, and one thing and another of similar nature are responsible for many a discontented home. A social-service meeting, an afternoon tea, a matinee, or whatnot, is no excuse for there being no dinner ready, time after time, when a husband comes home after a hard day's work. On the other hand, when a wife has carefully prepared a good meal, it is a heart-break to her and a positive injustice, when it is allowed to be spoiled, time after time, by the careless indifference of a husband who comes in an hour or two late.

Then (for the wife particularly) there is the very important matter of personal appearance. During courtship days you are always anxious to appear at your best on the nights when Prince Charming is going to be present. Don't think that such care is unnecessary after marriage. A good many women do think so. Yet how can a woman expect a man to be a constant admirer if, as soon as she is married, she ceases to do all the little things, simple and beautiful in themselves, that she used to think of in order to gain his admiration and love? Never allow yourself to drift into the frame of mind that says, "Oh, we're married now, so it doesn't matter." Believe me it does matter. Disaster lies down that road. Many little things are of more importance *after* marriage than before. In your courtship days he sees you at intervals only, and the romance of your presence and the newness of his passion blind him to the fact that the flowers at your neck, or the ribbon placed coyly in your hair, really do enhance your charm. But after you are married you will be daily companions in the stern battle of life, and the romantic glamour of your earliest love may wear thin *unless you are both careful to preserve it as the most beautiful thing in the world.*

In true marriage the bonds of your mutual love may

well grow stronger and stronger, but carelessness and indifference will soon weaken them. You will want your husband to fall in love with you every day, as he will surely want you to fall in love with him. Of course, you can't always be dressed up, but you can try to be always clean and neat, and you can welcome him always with a smile that comes so easy now. You will be tired, at times, with the labors and cares of the day; sickness may come upon you, and there may be days when the path will seem rough and hard; your purse may seem light; even the little comforts and luxuries of life which, perhaps, seem commonplace today, may be lacking; even the sting of poverty may be felt. If you have a true companionship with the man you love—a companionship grounded in mutual understanding and devotion and self-sacrifice—you will find yourself strong in the day of battle; and, what is of more importance, you will prove a source of strength and courage and inspiration to him in his conflict with the world. This is true marriage.

Again, avoid the mistake of thinking that success in life is to be measured by the quantity of your earthly possessions. It may be silly of me to proffer advice of this kind, for it belongs to a philosophy of life that I cannot assume you have yet attained. Still, if you are observant, even to the extent of noting the headlines in the daily papers, you will realize that fine houses, costly clothes, expensive cars, private yachts, winter homes in Florida, and all such things as these, do not by any means ensure happiness. If you could find the happiest people in the world, you would probably discover that they are fine souls not cluttered up with a great amount of earthly possessions. But this is no suggestion on my part that poverty, or insufficiency, is a virtue, or is to be desired. Very far from it. Poverty is a curse that is the result of the faulty system under which we live. Some day things will be changed, and under an equitable system of some kind or other, poverty will be abolished and all men and women will find a sufficiency of the good and fine things of life provided by their own contributions to the commonwealth. However, I must not digress into the fields of economics and politics. That is another story.

Housekeeping accomplishments and cooking ability are, of course, positive essentials in any true home, and every wife should take a reasonable pride in her skill. It is a libel to say that the only way to a man's heart is through his stomach, but it is very certain that a man's disposition (or a woman's) is largely a matter of good health, and good health is very largely a matter of correct diet, which means wholesome food and properly cooked meals. Happiness does not flourish in an atmosphere of dyspepsia.

But there are many more matters to consider. I would not for a moment suggest that the partner you are going to marry is not all that you think him, or her, to be; I am sure that your good common sense tells you that little failings on the part of both are likely to become apparent to each other when the daily life is lived under a colder and more penetrating light than is afforded by the honeymoon. Such revelations must be received with wisdom and forbearance. You will have taken each other "for better, for worse," and both of you must be prepared to make allowances. Don't expect too much from life. If there is mutual sympathy and understanding and the sustaining power of unselfish love which reaches to the mountain peaks of ecstasy as you lie in each other's arms, you may well be satisfied and say to yourselves, "the lot has fallen unto me in a fair ground."

SULKING

Whenever you have little differences and the tension for a moment becomes noticeable, *don't sulk*. Sulking is a home-destroying habit of the worst kind. And here is the place to interject a word of advice that I know to be very sound. Do not get into the habit of engaging in intercourse as a means of settling your differences. Wonderful as sexual intercourse is, it does not patch up fundamental differences. That is not its forte. Under the emotional stress of sexual feelings serious differences may be, and will be, forgotten for the moment. But they are not cured. There is only one satisfactory modus operandi when differences have disturbed your equanimity. Have a simple and straightforward unemotional talk, and try to thresh the matter out in a spirit of cool common sense and mutual sympathy. When that has been done satisfactorily, the sexual embrace may be engaged in to set a seal on your new understanding. You cannot afford to sulk with one another. You have to walk the path of life together and fight its battles side by side. Your mutual happiness, the welfare of your home and children, the worthwhile-ness of life itself, are, perhaps, in the balance. Don't sulk.

Again, avoid the first approach towards anything that in your past experience has led to argument or dispute. The wise mariner, having discovered a hidden rock that is a menace to his ship, puts a floating buoy over it, and then keeps as far away from the hidden danger as possible. Look ahead and be wise. I am not suggesting for a moment that you are not both entitled to perfect freedom in your personal views and opinions. Both partners have to realize that and learn to respect each other's rights. Constant disputes will destroy the happiness of any home, for they never lead anywhere but to the arid deserts of silence and sulkiness, and they tend to create an argumentative disposition that is not conducive to the well-being of a home.

NAGGING

And now I am going to direct your attention to one of the most dangerous rocks in the sea of matrimony. I am referring to the fatal habit of nagging. I verily believe that the happiness of homes is destroyed more frequently by the habit of nagging than by any other one thing. No home can survive it indefinitely. Of course, we men are often careless and clumsy, and do all sorts of things that we ought not do, and perhaps leave undone still more things that we ought to do, and all that. But there is a very excellent reason for it. The reason is that we are just men, and not arch-angels. A woman who takes pride in her house to such a degree that she practically worships it and the furniture in it and the waxed floors, and all the rest of the things which she spends most of her time keeping perfect and spotless, is certainly going to be provoked by an ordi-nary man-creature about the place who disarranges the cushions on her davenport, or leaves his pipe on the parlor table, or accidentally drops some cigar ashes on the floor. We ought, of course, to be ashamed of our slovenly shortcomings when we are guilty of such grievous infractions of the law of the queen-mother. Such law-givers, however, seem to overlook the fact that, to the simple male mind, houses are built, not that they may be kept spotlessly clean, but primarily to be homes for human beings.

There are some women who, by some sort of divine endowment, are able to keep their houses quite spotless enough to make them real homes, without making their husbands feel like criminals every day of the year. But —there are others. "John, I wish you wouldn't do that." "John, what on earth did you do that for?" "John, I wish you wouldn't leave your dirty old magazines on the couch." "John, just look at those tracks you've made on the waxed floor; you are the mussiest thing I ever saw." "John, I wish you wouldn't leave your old pipe on the mantelpiece"—and so on, every day with its full quota. And because the floors are waxed and shining, and the table-linen clean, and the beds spotless, the well-meaning but poor unfortunate wife imagines she has made a home for her husband that he ought to be proud of. As a matter of fact, he hasn't a home at all. He is just one of the millions of men for whom the word home may be defined as "a place where a man goes after business hours to be nagged at." A man may stand that sort of thing for a long time, but the chances are against his standing it permanently. If he needs peace to make life bearable, he will have to look for it elsewhere than in his own house. And it is quite likely that he will look.

PARENTS-IN-LAW

This world affords few things more beautiful than filial affection and devotion—the love of sons and daughters for their parents. "Honor thy father and thy mother" as a prescription for a long life "in the land of the living" may not be infallible, but certain it is that sons and daughters whose hearts are sincerely attached in honor and love to their parents, and who are deeply thoughtful of their happiness, demonstrate thereby their own worth and rightness. They are of the kind that are not likely to go far astray in life.

This love and sense of duty, however beautiful and commendable it may be, often results in conditions that tend to produce discord in the homes of young married couples. It is an elemental fact, discovered far back in prehistoric times, that mothers and fathers ought not to live with their married children, nor married children with their parents. Of course, there are occasions and circumstances, unfortunately, when such an arrangement may be unavoidable, but fundamentally it is not right, and more particularly so in the early years of a young couple's life.

A mother who has brought children into the world, and nurtured and taught and guarded and provided for them from infancy until marriage, finds it difficult to abdicate her place of authority in favor of either her own daughter, or, still worse, the daughter of some other woman. Presuming on her relationship and experience, she is very apt to interfere in matters that her good sense ought to tell her are really none of her business. If she is in her son's or daughter's home she should recognize it as *their* home, not hers, and no contribution she may make to the expenses of the home should affect her recognition and acceptance of this fact. If she has not sufficient means to provide for herself, her married children should, if possible, make whatever contributions may be necessary to provide her with what she needs. She should have her own establishment, and when she enters the home of a married son or daughter, it should be as a loved mother on a visit—not as a permanent addition to the household. This may sound a rather cold-blooded attitude, but I assure you it is very far from being that. The simple fact is that mothers in the home of a married son or daughter do not make for peace. Conflict in authority, resulting in a divided allegiance, is almost inevitable, and all sorts of trouble and discord are apt to arise in an atmosphere of that kind.

Of course, the mothers are always well-intentioned. That goes without saying. They see what they judge to be one thing after another being done wrongly, and their maternal instinct makes them fly to the rescue, not realizing that their act of rescue is very likely to be looked on as an interference. And it is interference. The advice of experience is always a valuable thing, and no young couple should scorn it. But tactful advice is one thing, and the assumption of maternal authority is another. When disputes arise (as they invariably do), "sides" inevitably develop in the situation, and that is almost certain to create bad feelings and unhappy conditions that have in them the seeds of disaster.

Young couples need to live together, with no call for any divided allegiance. It is an imposition for any husband to bring a mother into his wife's home and permit the mother to exercise any measure of household management. That kingdom belongs to the wife he has taken unto himself. It is an imposition for any wife tacitly to assume that her husband married her family as well as herself, and expect him to provide for them. There are times, of course, when the shelter of a home must be given to a needy parent, but in such circumstances it is the parent's part to be very tactful and accept the love and care that is being gladly extended, without venturing to offer the slightest authoritative interference. If the parent does not sense this obligation instinctively, the son or daughter should, in gentleness and sympathy, explain it without any equivocation.

I have written above more particularly about mothers-in-law in this connection, because they are the chief offenders. A father-in-law, should he come to the point of having to be cared for, is less likely to be obtrusive. A cosy corner with a newspaper and his pipe will probably satisfy him. At any rate he is not likely to bother about the running of the house.

The happiness of homes is being ruined every day by differences and quarrels springing from the inability of young couples to live their own lives. Love and honor your parents to the utmost, and your partner's parents, but remember that your wise love will be manifested in a higher degree by helping them, if your help is necessary, to live their own lives in a home of their cwn, rather than by forcing them into the environment of yours. They will be far happier, and so will you and your partner.

But, entirely apart from the question of relationship, it is a grave misfortune for a young couple to have to tolerate in their home the continual presence of *any third person whatsoever*. They invariably, and of necessity, find that a third party makes quite impossible the close, intimate, heart-to-heart life that marriage must be if it is to be successful. Even more after marriage than before, is it true that "two make company but three make a crowd." A young couple needs to feel the security of perfect privacy and their total dependence on each other—to be able to talk together on any and every subject without being conscious of someone else listening in; to be able to express their own ideas without fear of criticism from a third person; to be able to manifest their feelings at any time and in any way without fear of intrusion. With a third person under the same roof, sitting in on every conversation, there is always a sense of restriction, where absolute freedom of companionship is essential. This whole matter is one of very great importance and ought to be wisely guarded against.

MONEY

Another thing that should be discussed sanely and deliberately by every couple before marriage is the vital matter of money and the distribution of income. Avoid making the mistake of supposing that marriage is nothing but romance, and that to mention such things as money is next door to sacrilege. Money has a very direct bearing on the actual sexual life of a couple, for that life can come to its highest development only in an atmosphere of mutual happiness, and the money matters and arrangements of the house are frequently the source of feelings of dissatisfaction and of positive resentment; and such feelings are not conducive to love.

Next to actual disharmony in the matter of sex itself, the question of money is the shoal in the sea of matrimony on which most wrecks occur. Most of the young wives of today have at some time or other been wage-earners, and, as such, have had the pleasure and responsibility of spending their earnings to best advantage. They have developed a considerable degree of self-reliance, independence and common sense. Whenever they wanted anything, provided it was within the bounds of possibility, they would save towards that end, and would find a good deal of real satisfaction in eventually securing what they desired. But when they get married that life, with its adventures in finance, is apt to come to an end. The young wife finds herself in a new organization, in the role of partner—a role however which may have nothing whatever to do with the production of actual cash income. Any increase in her personal efforts as housewife will not increase the family budget. Unless she carries on some independent business activity, she is likely to find herself henceforward entirely dependent on an allowance from her husband. If she ever comes to feel that the allowance is unjust and inequitable, in view of what her husband spends on himself, the feeling is going to affect her attitude towards him, and that change of feeling is apt to lead on and on to disharmony and possible disaster.

The husband, of course, is usually the money-maker for the family, and technically he is the supporter of the home, but that is very far from being any reason why he should claim or desire dictatorial power over the whole income. Marriage, if it is to be successful in the highest degree, must be a partnership—not a dictatorship by the husband. He may earn the income that supports the home, yet he must remember that but for his wife he would have no home to support. He may work from eight or nine in the morning till five or six in the evening, but his wife has a good deal longer day than that; and her work is often far more wearying and monotonous than his. So long as she exercises reasonable care and common sense in her spending, she ought not to be compelled to go to her husband, like a panhandler, for every dime she needs. She has the house to take care of, the children and herself to dress, the table to provide for, and a hundred and one other minor matters that have to be taken care of, and generally she does it all with credit to herself. A true marriage must be a true partnership in which each has the same goal in view, in which each does his or her part, and all income belongs rightly to both. Discuss these matters together with common sense before you get married.

RELIGION

Religion, I am sorry to say, is very often a disturbing element in the home rather than the unifying influence that it ought to be. It ought to go without saying that young people of strong religious convictions that do not jibe ought *never* to get married to one another. A Roman Catholic husband who believes firmly that his church is the only true gateway into the kingdom of heaven, and that his wife and children ought to belong to it in order that they may be saved, is not going to be particularly happy with a strongly Protestant wife who very definitely believes nothing at all of the sort. An intelligent Unitarian wife could never have much respect for the mentality of a rigid fundamentalist husband to whom every word in the Bible is the inspired word of the peculiar God that he claims to believe in. An Anglican wife would never be happy with a Baptist husband who would refuse to have their children baptised in infancy, a practice that he considers wrong, while she (if she is a rigid and true Anglican) believes that it is necessary to their salvation. In all cases such as these dissension is bound sooner or later to spring up. It is a fortunate thing however that couples so far apart in their religious beliefs do not usually fall in love.

But there are more frequent differences than these, and usually they are the result of wrong religious concepts in the matter of sex. Some wives succeed in bringing themselves to the point where they believe (or profess to believe) that sex, in all its manifestations, is part of some "lower nature" in which their husbands are still grovelling, while they themselves have risen to some purer and more godly life. Such wives either refuse their husbands all sex-companionship, or else they submit themselves to it passively, as martyrs, and manifest in every possible way their disgust at the whole procedure. The moment an atmosphere of this kind envelops the marriage bed disaster settles over the home. Such a wife may rather confidently expect that, sooner or later, her husband is going to seek elsewhere for the sympathy and companionship that she promised when she married him, but which she sees fit to refuse.

Unfortunately there is not much hope in a situation of this kind. If, before the date of her marriage, a woman realizes that sex, as sex, has no appeal for her, and if she does not see quite clearly that it is essentially pure, and that its manifestations, growing out of true love, are deeply and truly sacred, she ought to call her marriage off and not deceive and blight the life of the man whom she ought to love as a man because she is a woman. As a matter of fact she is probably figuring on the marriage certificate to be a sort of free ticket for bed and board—the whole thing being a business matter, into which she is willing to enter under false pretences.

As an illustration of how extreme such cases are at times, I may give one from my own contact. A clergyman came to see me confessing that he was at about the limit of his endurance. He was about thirty-nine years of age and a robust and healthy man. He had been married about fourteen years. His wife was an attractive woman who took a real interest in his academic work and scholastic accomplishments. Friends considered them well mated and a happy couple. As a matter of fact up to the time he came to me he had never had any intercourse with his wife. He had approached her, of course, innumerable times over the course of fourteen years but without result. She apparently had only one reason for this most extraordinary attitude—"I don't think it is nice." In this particular case the advice I was able to give to the disturbed husband brought about a better state of affairs, and as I have not heard anything to the contrary I hope their home is a happier place.

To every couple with any differences in their religious beliefs I beg to offer my personal conclusions for whatever they may be worth: The differences between the various churches, as far as forms and ceremonies are concerned, are not worth one minute of argument or dissension. All the creeds were made by men, and men only, and for the most part by men whose names even we do not know, who certainly had no more authority to impose their views on the world than you or I would have. The conflicts in their differing creeds have been a very great curse to the world, for, as every historian knows, they have been the sad and terrible cause of more suffering, sorrow, persecution, and bloody wars than any other one thing.

Religion, as it has been visualized and demonstrated by the greatest souls that have ever lived, with Jesus of Nazareth at their head, is just what He showed it to be— a life of love and kindness and sympathy that knows no difference between nationalities, creeds, classes or color. If you want to love "God," the only possible way you can do it is to love your fellow-men. Humanity is the great host of souls, men, women, children, that has emerged from the silent past, and that is plodding on towards the mysterious silence ahead. The road is hard for many, and hope languishes, and sorrow stalks by their side; and our most beautiful acts in life are those that help and strengthen and make happier the companions who have grown weary and who stumble by the way. We do not need to trouble much about theologies—*"Inasmuch as ye have done it unto one of the least of these, ye have done it unto Me."*

An old Hebrew prophet gave a definition of religion that will stand for all time: "For what doth the Lord require of thee but to do justly, to love mercy, and to walk humbly before God." If we all lived that religion in home and State, the world's problems would be solved.

"UNFAITHFULNESS"

The matter of unfaithfulness, whenever its existence is suspected by either husband or wife, is, of course, a major factor in the unhappiness and wreckage of homes. The divorce cases where adultery is the charge testify to that fact without any doubt.

This book is intended to be a guide to brides-to-be and their fiances, and it cannot be extended into a philosophical, historical or moral disquisition on the many-sided question of marriage in its social aspects. The simple fact is that in our form of civilization no normal wife views with equanimity the sight of her husband succumbing to the allurement of another woman, and, needless to say, husbands feel the same way in regard to their wives and other men. Sexual jealousy has existed from away back, and is going to continue for some time to come.

All I can do in a book of this nature is to make two or three suggestions which, if observed, will certainly help to avoid conditions out of which a considerable amount of "unfaithfulness" arises.

First. A man must find the roof under which he dwells—be it a palace or a cottage, a rented house, an apartment, or even a single room—a real home where he can have the congenial companionship of a loving wife in an atmosphere that he can enjoy when the day's work is done. Some wives have the faculty of making such a home; some unfortunately have not. One of the most important matters with which a girl who is going to get married can occupy herself is the consideration of what kind of home she intends (so far as lies in her power) to create for the man she intends to companion through life. It will be his duty to provide the means; it will be her duty to build up the best home she can on such means as are available. The love of a man for his home with its atmosphere of contentment is at least one anchor (and a strong one) calculated to keep him there.

Second. Think of the following suggestions and their implications very carefully. Suppose a wife, expecting her husband's arrival from business, has prepared dinner for him. Marketing in the morning, she remembered his choice of meat and was careful to get an extra-fine cut, and she has cooked it to a turn. The vegetables are such as he likes. The soup and salad have been matters of concern to her, and she has been successful throughout. She has taken special care in the arrangement of the table—her best cutlery and dishes and finest linen are all in evidence, and a little colorful decoration is tastefully displayed. All that she has done has been a loving joy to her, and she is looking forward to the meal as much as he is. She has guarded her strength through the day and has no touch of weariness, and as he comes into the house she greets him with a smile of welcome and a touch of manifest love.

Now I submit that it would be absurdly impossible to suppose that that man, hungry, seeing the attractiveness of everything, would ever turn his back on the exquisite meal provided for him and leave the house, and by choice go off to some restaurant where he would not even be quite sure of the quality of the food that would be served. Such action would be simply unthinkable. But if the wife, though amply supplied with funds, is constantly setting him down to indigestible meals, cold and unappetizing, with nothing properly cooked, set out on the kitchen table with a dirty cloth, she need not be surprised if her husband frequently telephones from the office that business will prevent him from being home for dinner, and that he will just get a "snack" down town. As a matter of fact, he is probably staying down town so that he can get a bit of something decent to eat, for a change. And it is too often just the same with his sex life.

But one of the points I have been striving to make in

this book is that such conditions need not exist. There is no form of caress known to any mistress or courtesan that is not a perfectly legitimate possession of every wife. As a matter of fact, there is no form of caress that would not come naturally to any woman who has freed herself from unwholesome repressions and inhibitions. The normal, healthy and loving wife is quite able to make the sex experience of herself and her husband exquisitely entrancing. Seeing sex as an essentially vital function making for health of mind and body, and the source of ecstatic pleasure, she can throw herself into her sexual seances with her husband with a joyful abandon that will leave him very certain that he is married to the most wonderful woman on earth. Husbands are not likely to seek other pastures when those at home are so exquisite. To stray elsewhere means considerable expense, the danger of disease to himself which he may communicate later to his wife and children, and the certainty of unhappiness in his home—if not its destruction.

I am not suggesting for one instant that all marital unhappiness and subsequent unfaithfulness of husbands with mistresses and prostitutes springs solely from sexual insufficiency on the part of wives. I have enumerated many factors that go to the making of happiness and unhappiness in the home, but I am quite certain that sexual disharmony is the main cause, and in this statement I am borne out by the judges of our divorce courts and all others who have had opportunity to form opinions on the subject. Moreover, it is a fact that an unsatisfactory sex life makes both men and women irritable, and consequently minor matters are apt to develop into disputes when they would otherwise be passed over with little or no concern. In short, if a man finds sexual joy, par excellence, at home it will tend to maintain health of body and mind and the happiness of all life beneath his roof, and it will be, as I have already stated, quite unlikely that, at the cost of money and the danger of disease and the impairment of his faculties, he will seek an inferior quality elsewhere.

The substance of what I have written above, along with all its implications, is one of the most important matters in the world for the consideration of every wife. *The wives of the world have the morality and health and welfare of the world very much in their keeping.* Prostitution with its menace of unhappy homes and devastating diseases has blighted civilization too long, but it will never die out until the spontaneity and the abandon, the unrepressed desires of the body, the love of bodily exposure, the joyous and sensuous love-play, all of which have characterized the outsider's stock in trade, have been transferred to the home where they legitimately belong, and where they can serve only to bind husband and wife more closely together. The false education and absurd religious idealism that strive to banish sensual love from its due place in the hearts of normal men and women are being repudiated today more and more by common sense and true religion. Vital radiant passion is, and ever will be, the keynote to the truly happy home and *in proportion as it is, prostitution will die out and the world become happier and healthier.*

In mathematical terminology, prostitution and happy homes are in inverse proportion to one another. But a truly happy home can never be established without its proper foundation of sex, and the realization of its essential rightfulness, and the legitimacy of its demands, and the exquisiteness of the joys associated with it. No prostitute can ever compete with the wise wife for the simple reason that her heart knows no love for the man with whom she does business. It is a commercial proposition with her, and all her manifestations of passion are nothing but camouflage. She knows nothing of the sexual joy and ecstasy that it is the unrepressed wife's privilege to enjoy: her body is prostrated too frequently for that. But she is wise in the knowledge of *what sexual experiences ought to be,* and it is that which she sells —not love. But the wife, devoted to her husband, can well know all that there is to know—indeed it will be her *natural endowment* if she has banished hurtful repression and inhibition—and she will manifest her knowledge in an ocean of love. *There can be no competition with that.*

CONCLUSION

The path of vital sexual experience is the path that God has ordained that all His creatures shall tread. He has made them male and female. And He has made the path one of positive joy where love may reign, and where ardent desire may be ever aroused and be ever satisfied. Unfortunately, however, erroneous teaching, with a misconception of righteousness, looking askance at God's gift, has dug pitfalls on the path into which innumerable couples fall headlong because they have had no friend to warn and guide. In this book I have striven to be such a friend to any in need. I have tried to strip from our concepts of sex all the prudish habiliments that have tended to make a mystery of it—something hidden, something to be glanced at askance, something the very mention of which must be taboo. Instead I have tried to emphasize its naturalness, have reiterated its rightness and essential purity, and have shown it as a thing of which you do not need to be ashamed, but which you can delight in, and enjoy as the chief physical joy that God has given us—the source of much of the best and highest in life. Of course, like everything beautiful and sacred, it can be, and often is, desecrated; but the desecration almost always is the result of ignorance, coupled with the evil social and economic conditions of life that have interfered with the normal functioning of sex. Sooner or later all these things will be changed and better conditions will bring a saner and nobler understanding of life generally.

But while giving sex its due place I have laid stress on marriage as a life-long companionship, in which two personalities join forces to face the many problems of life. Such companionship, if it is to continue in mutual

145

happiness through the years until "death doth you part," must have other stones in the foundation besides the physical one of sex. You must consider those other stones with care. I have dealt with most of them briefly, of necessity, but sufficiently to suggest their importance.

But, after all, the chief cornerstone of happy marriage is romantic love that comes to its culmination in sexual joy. So if you would get all from your marriage that nature makes possible, and that God expects you to get, you must see sex in its true light and be as unrepressed and uninhibited in your attitude towards it, and in your enjoyment of it, as you are in the case of food when you are hungry. In every fiber of your being you must realize the essential purity of ardent sexual desire, its naturalness, its complete wholesomeness and your own inalienable right to all it may possess for you and your life partner.

Time after time we have heard that "Love is the fulfilling of the Law." That is something more than a religious platitude; it is a truth that has a deeper and wider significance and application than is often attached to it. It is really a comprehensive though rhetorical statement of the universal law of attraction, without which the universe itself would cease to be. In the realm of physics and chemistry atoms attract certain atoms to form molecules which, in turn, attract other molecules to form the infinite compounds that constitute the material world. In the biological realm, male and female are attracted to one another, and on that attraction, and the sexual union that naturally follows, depends the continuation of the life of the world. In our own human division of that life, physical love may, and should, and often does, rise to the heights of devotion, and breathes there an atmosphere where self is forgotten, and where one's very life, without the thought of sacrifice, would be gladly laid down for the object of our love. "Greater love hath no man than this."

Love, the bright jewel, has many facets from all of which some glorifying light streams forth on the path of life, redeeming it from its grayness. There is the love of truth, the love of beauty, the love of justice, the love of mercy, the great wide love of humanity, parental love and filial love. If mankind could be converted to worship with heart and soul and mind and body at the shrine of truth and beauty and love, and all that those terms imply, we should find, overnight, that our worship had ushered in the kingdom of God.

Wherever true love is found it is beautiful. Romantic love that has its roots in mutual admiration, and that is sustained and strengthened by understanding, thoughtfulness and sympathy, and that manifests itself in tender solicitude and protective care, and that reaches the mountain peaks of ecstasy in the lovers' embrace— an embrace that ultimates in a new life being brought into the world upon which maternal and paternal love bestows itself in willing sacrifice—that is a very beautiful thing indeed; a thing on which the very life of the world today, and in the future, is contingent.

"Love Is the Fulfilling of the Law."

147

A Few Questions That Are Often Asked, And The Answers

Should girls under twenty-one get married?

A girl may be fully developed physically by the time she is eighteen, and there are many marriages that turn out well with girls as young as this. But the fact remains that a girl of twenty-one is generally more emotionally stable, and less likely to make an unwise choice in a husband. When a girl marries at twenty-one, but delays pregnancy for a couple of years during which she and her husband are developing in mutual understanding and companionship, we may consider the prospects as good as possible from the point of view of age.

Is menstruation always painful?

No, but unfortunately most women do suffer more or less. Sometimes a surgical stretching of the cervix and curetting of the uterus make things better. The customary monthly distress often disappears after motherhood has been attained. Attention to diet, proper exercise and regular daily habits may help. Where the monthly discomfort is pronounced, a doctor should be consulted.

Should bathing be given up during menstruation?

Complete body-bathing will do no harm if the room is quite comfortable and the water warm. Avoid extremes of heat and cold. During this period a woman should wash herself locally several times a day. Some women tolerate even outside bathing in cold water with no harm.

Is sexual intercourse harmful during menstruation?

A woman's sexual organs are congested during the menstrual flow and care is desirable about sexual stimulation. It was formerly taught that intercourse might make the man suffer some local irritation unless he used a sheath, but this is no longer recognized as being a fact. There is a distinct esthetic feeling against it in some women.

The objection is mostly old taboo, and some women have strong desire at this time. Attention, however, may be directed to the reference to this matter on page 50.

Is complete sexual abstinence natural?

Provided ordinary health is enjoyed by both husband and wife, and there is no incompatibility between them, sexual abstinence is unnatural. If it is found easily possible to abstain for long periods, it indicates not high spiritual ideals (which may coexist with a full and wholesome sex life) but weak sex impulses. If, because of some false religious idea or silly theory, it is persisted in despite urgent desire, it is apt to eventuate in some psychical or physiological disturbance.

Is there a "safe" period for wives?

The "safe-period" method is known also as the "rhythm" method. According to this theory, the safe period, in a woman with a twenty-eight-day menstrual cycle, would be about eighteen days in the month —from about ten days before, until about eight or nine days after, the start of menstruation. There is another way of determining the safe period that is today regarded as more accurate. That is by basal-temperature testing, to determine the time of ovulation. If the temperature is taken each day immediately upon waking and noted on a chart, there will be seen a rise in temperature at about the same time each month. This marks the time of ovulation, usually about the fourteenth day preceding the start of the next menstrual period. At ovulation and for perhaps several days afterward, the woman is fertile; those women who wish to practice the "safe-period" method will refrain from intercourse during this time (and for a day or two preceding ovulation). However, since the menstrual cycle is irregular with most women and dependent on many factors, the "safe-period" is not always easy to calculate; and the method should by no means be regarded as completely reliable.

Is the ability to have children an essential to marriage?

No. No person, however, should become engaged knowing of any inability to have children, without making the fact known to the other person. If there is a complete mutual acceptance of the situation, marriage may, of course, be undertaken.

Is it possible for pregnancy to occur without penetration?

Yes. The sperms from the male are very active. If they come in contact with the moist vaginal opening it is possible for them to work their way up the passage, and pregnancy may possibly result.

How soon is life felt after pregnancy has occurred?

About the end of the fifth month.

Is childbirth very painful?

Medical science has advanced to such a degree that childbirth need not be dreaded. The early pains are not generally severe. When they become more pronounced anesthetics can be administered which relieve the woman of the worst suffering without interfering with the natural muscular contractions.

What is a "Caesarean" birth?

When normal birth is impossible for certain reasons, the surgeon makes an incision in the abdomen and then into the uterus, and through this incision the child is brought into the world. With modern technique and special skill there is a low degree of danger in this operation.

How long should a baby be nursed at the breast?

Not longer than nine months. The milk of a healthy mother is, of course, the best food in the world for an infant, but the weaning should not be deferred beyond nine months. Too prolonged nursing tends to produce rickets and other troubles in an infant.

How soon after childbirth may the sex life be resumed?

When a healthy mother has a normal labor her sex organs will have fully recovered in five or six weeks. In order that she may make a perfect recovery, sexual intercourse should not be resumed earlier than this.

Can a mother become pregnant while she is nursing a baby?

Yes. Many a woman knows only too well from repeated experiences that she may have to take care of two of her progeny at the same time—one in her arms and one in her uterus.

What is meant by a "Companionate Marriage"?

Marriage is always an adventure, the outcome of which can never be foreseen. If, in the course of a few months or years, the couple find that they are mismated, disappointed, and unhappy, they are doomed to that life-long misery under our present laws, unless they obtain a divorce. But divorces are difficult and costly things to get, and they cannot be obtained by mutual consent. In Canada and some other places adultery has to be proved by the offended partner. Needless to say, there is collusion in lots of divorce cases. Judge Lindsay of Denver has suggested what he terms "companionate marriage" as a solution to this desperately bad state of affairs. Companionate marriage would mean a perfectly legal marriage in which birth control would be practiced until such time as the couple were satisfied that they were properly mated, and were ready to make their marriage permanent by raising a family. Up to that time, however, if they found themselves unhappy together, a simple form of divorce could be obtained by mutual consent and both would then be free to make a fresh start.

Is it right for anyone to marry if there is a history of venereal disease?

The venereal diseases are gonorrhea and syphilis. Gonorrhea is a localized disease of the sexual organs, painful, at times serious, very contagious, but not inheritable. Communicated to the eyes of a child at the time of birth it may cause blindness. Under a doctor's treatment gonorrhea can be cured, but no sexual relationship must be indulged in until a thorough examination reveals no trace of the disease.

Syphilis is an exceedingly serious disease—a real blood infection. If proper medical treatment is secured from the earliest stages a cure may usually be effected—often rapidly—but only with obedience and cooperation on the part of the patient. If the disease is allowed to progress far without attention a cure may never be brought about. Patience and medical skill may eradicate all trace of the condition and

152

then marriage is considered as justified. The doctor must be the judge.

Is it wrong for first cousins to marry?

Not necessarily so. When cousins marry it is, of course, a matter of inbreeding if they have children. Inbreeding, however, is not necessarily harmful. All scientific florists, agriculturists and stock-raisers have to depend on inbreeding for the production of their finest varieties and strains. Intelligent selection, however, is needed in the process. Undesirable traits can be as easily produced as desirable ones. When cousins wish to marry, the health histories of both families should be very carefully investigated by a doctor. If both family histories should happen to reveal a common hereditary, mental or physical defect, the marriage should be very definitely discouraged. If a clean bill of hereditary health can be found, there is no argument against the union. If love has already established itself between the couple too deeply to be uprooted with impunity, and at the same time hereditary conditions are not favorable, then sterilization would be a possible solution.

What is sterilization?

Sterilization is a surgical operation that is performed on either a man or a woman in order that pregnancy may not occur as a result of their sexual activities. While the best birth-control methods are extremely efficient (very close to 100% if care and intelligence are used), still there are cases where absolutely no risk whatever would be permissible—for instance, where pregnancy in all probability would result in death. In such cases it does not mean that marriage must be forbidden or sexual life prohibited. Sterilization is a solution to such a problem.

For a man this operation is a very minor affair that can be attended to in the doctor's office under a local anesthetic. It is a matter of only a few minutes, and after it is over, the man can go about his ordinary work in a day or two without any inconvenience. The operation consists of cutting and tying two small tubes called the vasa deferentia (see illustration on page 37) which are very close to the surface and can be reached through incisions not more than half an inch in length.

This operation does not affect a man's sexual powers so far as intercourse with his wife is concerned—his climax is reached and his ejaculation occurs just the same—the only result is, that his wife will never become pregnant.

For the wife the operation is a much more serious one that necessitates ten days or two weeks in a hospital, opening the abdomen and then tying the Fallopian tubes (see illustration on page 33) that lead from the ovaries to the uterus. With a skilled surgeon the operation is practically without danger. Sterilization in man or woman has no undesirable or injurious results physically or mentally. Being a certain guarantee against pregnancy, it may be expected to increase the happiness of homes where fears have produced trouble.

Sterilization for mentally deficient or unfit persons has been definitely legalized in twenty-nine states of the United States and tens of thousands of operations have been reported. It is legalized also in British Columbia and in the Province of Alberta and a movement is being made to have a similar law passed in Ontario.

From the above description of sterilization it ought not to be necessary to say that it is a totally different thing from castration. Castration means the total removal of the testicles in a man or of the ovaries in a woman. This explanation is added because some apparently quite intelligent people confound the two operations. No normal man would consent to castration, but many men who have no intention, under any circumstances, of fathering any more children, are applying for sterilization so that there may be no further anxiety on that score.

Are mechnical devices, made of gold or silver, that are inserted in the uterus for contraceptive purposes, to be recommended?

Very emphatically—*no*. The uterus is a very delicate part of a woman's anatomy and any possible cause of irritation should be avoided.

Should married couples sleep together or are twin beds preferable?

If they are reasonably healthy they should sleep together as they have been doing from the beginning of time. Twin beds may easily turn out to be the first step to the door of the divorce court. Marie Stopes has termed them an invention of the devil. Making allowances for her figurative language, I agree with her.

INDEX

A

Abortion, dangers of, 55-57
  therapeutic, 56
Autoerotism, 106-110, 117
  masturbation, 106-110

B

Babies, come from where, 40-41
Birth control, 47, 56, 58-66
  and fear of pregnancy, 58
  by contraceptives, 62
  in marital failure, 60
Body odor, 67
Bridal night, the, 90-95

C

Cervix, or neck of the uterus, or womb, 32
Chapple, Harold, 57
Childbirth, 33
Circumcision, 36
Climax, *see* orgasm
Clitoris, the, 31, 32, 76, 85, 99
  hooded, 118
Coital fluid, 83
Coitus, positions for, 96-102
"Coitus reservatus," 103-105
  danger of pregnancy in, 104
  love-play in, 103
  lubrication, need of, 103
Contraceptives, use of, 62

D

Dawson of Penn, Lord, xiii
Deaths caused by abortion, 55
Detumescence, 102
Douching, 81
Duration of period of intercourse, the, 86

E

Early marriages versus long engagements, 65-66
  and birth control, 66
Ejaculate, the amount of, 38
Ejaculation, 87, 99
Ellis, Havelock, xiii, 108
Engagements, long, versus early marriages, 65-66
  and birth control, 66
Erection, 35
Erogenous zones in woman's body, the, 75-76
Erotic conversation, 79

F

Fallopian tubes, 33
False religious idealism, 27
First night, the, 90-95
  and the hymen, 94
Foreskin, or prepuce, the, 36
Frequency of intercourse, 44-47

A few typical comments regarding previous editions of this work.

"In the day's work of a physician there is a definite place for this book. It is the one to recommend to those people who have been raised in churchly homes where all sex impulses . . . are looked at askance."—*Ohio State Medical Journal.*

"It is one of the best books of advice produced and the fact that it appears under the aegis of a minister will make it valuable where there is a religious conflict."—*American Journal of Orthopsychiatry.*

"A practical handbook of sexual information to enable couples to achieve normal, happy marriage; intended for those married or about to be."—*Journal of Home Economics.*

"A frank and complete description of all aspects of marital relations, written in a very sympathetic style. Simple yet authoritative material."
—*Child Study Association.*

"Meets the need particularly of people reared in any church teaching or home atmosphere that looks askance at sex impulses. It fills a need for a simple form of instruction. The wording of it is such that as sex education or medical information stated in terms suitable to the laity, no one could, in my opinion, take exception to it.

"My familiarity with the literature on this subject allows me to make a comparison, and in doing so I feel that [this book] is restrained and moderate and embodies the information essential to a happy marital adjustment."—*Robert L. Dickinson, M.D.* (*New York*).

"In every way the book is direct, simple and wise, and gives excellent and sane advice about anatomy, physiology, contraception, intercourse and mild sexual disturbances."—*The Psychoanalytic Quarterly.*

"Sound medical popularization . . . written in simple language."
—*American Sociological Review.*

159

"This is a thoroughly worth-while book for the physician, and especially for him to recommend to his married and about-to-be-married patients and friends."—*Clinical Medicine and Surgery.*

"The book . . . is characterized by good sense."—*Paul Popenoe,* in *Public Health Nursing.*

"The author has succeeded in producing a complete manual for married happiness. It is an ideal present for the conscientious preacher to give to couples who come to him for the marriage ceremony."—*G. Raymond Booth, Friends' Church, Toronto.*

"While it is true that there is a vast array of volumes on Sex, and Marriage, most of them are either too ponderous and expensive, or too cheap and shoddy. [This book] strikes a happy and perfect medium. It is comprehensive yet concise; it is searching and serious, yet simple; it is scientific, yet human and warm. I heartily and unhesitatingly recommend it as filling a long-felt and most pressing need."—*Rabbi Maurice N. Eisendrath, Holy Blossom Synagogue, Toronto.*

[From a letter to the author] "Will you allow another minister (of the United Church) to congratulate you upon your book? It is brief, succinct, clear, straight, very sensible, Christian, most salutary. I would endorse every word you have written."—*Jas. F. McCurdy, B.A. (Ontario).*

"In our work we see so many people rendered unhappy because of poor sex adjustment that I am pleased to find a book at last containing the vital information, and at the same time selling for a very moderate price."—*J. D. Griffin, M.D., The Canadian National Committee for Mental Hygiene.*

"The author, an ardent and sincere crusader . . . describes with completeness and frankness the marital relations in their many aspects."—*The Canadian Doctor (Medical Journal).*

"An eminently sane and sound study deserving of warm recommendation. . . . Does not shun any detail that merits intelligent consideration."—*Montreal Star.*